Global Trade in Fakes

A WORRYING THREAT

This work is published under the responsibility of the Secretary-General of the OECD and the Executive Director of the EUIPO. The opinions expressed and arguments employed herein do not necessarily reflect the official views of the OECD member countries or the European Union Intellectual Property Office.

This document, as well as any data and map included herein, are without prejudice to the status of or sovereignty over any territory, to the delimitation of international frontiers and boundaries and to the name of any territory, city or area.

The names of countries and territories and territorial disclaimers used in this joint publication follow the practice of the OECD.

Note by Turkey
The information in this document with reference to "Cyprus" relates to the southern part of the Island. There is no single authority representing both Turkish and Greek Cypriot people on the Island. Turkey recognises the Turkish Republic of Northern Cyprus (TRNC). Until a lasting and equitable solution is found within the context of the United Nations, Turkey shall preserve its position concerning the "Cyprus issue".

Note by all the European Union Member States of the OECD and the European Union
The Republic of Cyprus is recognised by all members of the United Nations with the exception of Turkey. The information in this document relates to the area under the effective control of the Government of the Republic of Cyprus.

Please cite this publication as:
OECD/EUIPO (2021), *Global Trade in Fakes: A Worrying Threat*, Illicit Trade, OECD Publishing, Paris, *https://doi.org/10.1787/74c81154-en*.

ISBN 978-92-64-31330-9 (print)
ISBN 978-92-64-81302-1 (pdf)

Illicit Trade
ISSN 2617-5827 (print)
ISSN 2617-5835 (online)

European Union
ISBN 978-92-9156-297-8 (pdf)
Catalogue number Catalogue TB-03-21-308-EN-N (pdf)

Preface

Illicit trade in counterfeit and pirated goods poses a major challenge to an innovation-driven global economy. It damages economic growth; poses significant threats to individual and collective health and safety; fuels organised crime; undermines sound public governance, the rule of law and citizens' trust in government; and can, ultimately, threaten democracy and political stability. The COVID-19 pandemic has accelerated illicit trade, alarming law enforcement in many parts of the world.

Policy makers need solid empirical evidence for taking action against this threat. To meet this need, the OECD and the EU Intellectual Property Office (EUIPO) have joined forces to carry out a series of analytical studies. The results have been published in a set of reports that gauge illicit trade in counterfeit and pirated goods.

We are very pleased to provide an update on the quantitative results published in the 2016, and 2019 OECD – EUIPO reports. We are confident that the results will enhance our understanding of the risk that counterfeiting poses to the global economy, facilitate the development of innovative policy options to respond to these challenges, and promote clean trade in the post-COVID recovery.

Christian Archambeau,

Executive Director,

EUIPO

Elsa Pilichowski,

Director,

OECD, Public Governance Directorate

Foreword

Illicit trade in fake goods is a significant and growing threat in a globalised and innovation-driven economy. Its damaging effects on governance, innovation, the rule of law and, ultimately, on democracy cannot be underestimated.

In recent years the OECD and the EU Intellectual Property Office (EUIPO) have been collecting evidence on various aspects of this risk. The results have been published in a set of reports starting with *Trade in Counterfeit and Pirated Goods: Mapping the Economic Impact* (2016). These results have since been expanded and updated in subsequent reports, including *Mapping the Real Routes of Trade in Fake Goods* (2017) and *Trends in Trade in Counterfeit and Pirated Goods* (2019). The present report uses a tailored, statistical methodology, originally developed for a 2008 OECD study. It provides an update using the most recent data (from 2019) on trade in counterfeit goods. It also provides a snapshot of recent trends under the COVID-19 pandemic, based on a set of in-depth online dialogues and structured interviews with experts from enforcement and industry communities. Such an update is critical; not only for better understanding this threat, but also for developing effective governance responses to support post-COVID recovery.

The results are a cause for concern. Trade in counterfeit and pirated goods amounted to up to 2.5 % of world trade in 2019; when considering only imports into the EU, fake goods amounted to up to 5.8 % of imports. These amounts are similar to those of previous years, and illicit trade in fakes remains a serious risk to modern, open and globalised economies.

Counterfeiters misuse modern logistical solutions and legitimate trade facilitation mechanisms, and thrive in economies lacking good governance standards. The COVID-19 pandemic has intensified the problem: criminal networks have reacted very quickly to the crisis and adapted their strategies to take advantage of the shifting landscape.

This study was carried out under the auspices of the OECD's Task Force on Countering Illicit Trade, which focuses on evidence-based research and advanced analytics to assist policy makers in mapping and understanding the vulnerabilities exploited and created by illicit trade.

Acknowledgements

This report was prepared by the OECD Public Governance Directorate, under the leadership of Elsa Pilichowski, Public Governance Director and Martin Forst, Head of the Governance Reviews and Partnerships division, together with the European Union Intellectual Property Office (EUIPO), under the leadership of Christian Archambeau, Executive Director, and Paul Maier, Director of the European Observatory on Infringements of Intellectual Property Rights.

At the OECD this study was conducted under the auspices of the Task Force on Countering Illicit Trade (TF-CIT). The study was shared with other OECD committees with relevant expertise in the area of trade, regulatory policy, and public sector integrity.

The report was prepared by Piotr Stryszowski, Senior Economist and Morgane Gaudiau, Economist at the OECD Directorate for Public Governance jointly with Michał Kazimierczak, Economist at the European Observatory on Infringements of Intellectual Property Rights of the EUIPO and Nathan Wajsman, Chief Economist, EUIPO. The authors wish to thank the OECD experts who provided valuable knowledge and insights: Julio Bacio Terracino, and Nick Malyshev from the OECD Public Governance Directorate, and Silvia Sorescu from the OECD Trade Directorate.

The authors would also like to thank experts from the OECD member countries and participants of several seminars and workshops for their valuable assistance. Special expressions of appreciation are given to Riikka Pakkanen from Finnish Customs, George Agius from Malta Customs as well as to Phil Lewis from the UK Anti-Counterfeiting Group.

Raquel Páramo and Andrea Uhrhammer provided editorial and production support.

The database on customs seizures was provided by the World Customs Organization (WCO) and supplemented with regional data submitted by the European Commission's Directorate-General for Taxation and Customs Union, the US Customs and Border Protection Agency and the US Immigration and Customs Enforcement. The authors express their gratitude for the data and for the valuable support of these institutions.

Table of contents

Tables

Figures

Boxes

Follow OECD Publications on:

http://twitter.com/OECD_Pubs

http://www.facebook.com/OECDPublications

http://www.linkedin.com/groups/OECD-Publications-4645871

http://www.youtube.com/oecdilibrary

OECD Alerts http://www.oecd.org/oecddirect/

Executive Summary

This study presents an updated quantitative analysis of the value, scope and magnitude of world trade in counterfeit and pirated products. Based on data for 2019, it estimates that the volume of international trade in counterfeit and pirated products amounted to as much as USD 464 billion in that year, or 2.5% of world trade.

In previous OECD-EUIPO studies, which relied on the same methodology, trade in counterfeit and pirated goods was estimated at up to 2.5 % of world trade in 2013, equivalent to up to USD 461 billion, and 3.3% of world trade in 2016, or USD 509 billion. Thus, in nominal terms, in absolute terms and in terms of its share in total trade, the volume of trade in fakes has remained significant, representing amounts close to the GDPs of advanced OECD economies such as Austria or Belgium.

Drawing on detailed EU data, this study also provides an in-depth assessment of the situation in the European Union. The results show that in 2019, imports of counterfeit and pirated products into the EU amounted to as much as EUR 119 billion (USD 134 billion), which represents up to 5.8 % of EU imports. It should be noted that these results rely on customs seizure observations and do not include domestically produced and consumed counterfeit and pirated products; nor do they include pirated digital content on the Internet.

Counterfeiting and piracy threaten a large number of industries. Fakes can be found among many types of goods, including common consumer products (clothing, footwear), business-to-business products (spare parts, pesticides), and luxury items (fashion apparel, deluxe watches). Importantly, many fake goods can pose serious health, safety and environmental risks. These include fake pharmaceuticals in particular, but also food, cosmetics, toys, medical equipment and chemicals.

While counterfeit and pirated goods originate from virtually all economies in all continents, China remains the primary economy of origin.

Counterfeit and pirated products continue to follow complex trading routes, misusing a set of intermediary transit points. Many of these transit economies, for example Hong-Kong (China), Singapore or United Arab Emirates, are well developed, high-income economies and important hubs of international trade.

Fake goods tend to be shipped by every means of transport. In terms of the number of seizures, small parcels -- in particular via postal services -- is the most common, posing a significant challenge in terms of enforcement. In terms of value, counterfeits transported by container ship clearly dominate, accounting for more than a half of the global value of counterfeit seizures in 2019.

The COVID-19 pandemic has affected trade in fake goods, although, in terms of volume, the impact was smaller than initially expected. In most cases, the crisis has aggravated existing trends. The main trend was the intense misuse of the online environment. Under confinement, consumers turn to online markets to fulfil their needs, driving significant growth in the online supply of a wide range of counterfeits. The sharp increase in fakes concerned not only medicines and personal protective equipment (PPE), but many other goods, including watches, consumer goods, and products in the mechanical and electrical engineering and metalworking industry (e.g., kitchen appliances).

The analysis presented in this report is based primarily on a quantitative assessment using the tailored statistical methodologies developed by the OECD, drawing on data from a large dataset on customs seizures of intellectual property-infringing goods. The data refer to the pre-COVID period; the crisis has introduced a great deal of dynamism, and no final, robust conclusions as to the effects of the pandemic can be drawn at this stage.

To understand and combat the risk of counterfeit and pirated trade of trade in fakes, governments need up-to-date information on its magnitude, scope and trends. This study is part of a continuous monitoring effort to support policy and enforcement solutions.

Chapter 1. The trade in fakes: Setting the scene

Introduction

Globalisation, policies for improving trade facilitation and the rising economic importance of intellectual assets are important drivers of economic growth. These intangible assets in the global context have shifted the attention of industry and policymakers to intellectual property (IP). For modern industries, IP is one of the key value generators and enablers of success in competitive markets, and for policymakers it plays a crucial role in promoting innovation and driving sustained economic growth.

However, this rising importance of IP in the globalised world has created new opportunities for criminal networks to free ride on others' intellectual assets and pollute trade routes with counterfeits. The recently observed broadening scope and magnitude of counterfeiting, in particular in the context of trade, is seen as a significant economic threat that undermines innovation and hampers economic growth.

In order to provide policymakers with reliable empirical evidence on this threat, the Organisation for Economic Co-operation and Development (OECD) and the European Union Intellectual Property Office (EUIPO) joined forces to develop an understanding of the scale and magnitude of the problem of IP infringement in international trade. The results published in a series of reports that provided a general overview of this threat: Trade in Counterfeit and Pirated Goods: Mapping the Economic Impact (OECD/EUIPO, 2016[1]), Mapping the Real Routes of Trade in Fake Goods (OECD/EUIPO, 2017[2]) and Trends in Trade in Counterfeit and Pirated Goods (OECD/EUIPO, 2019[3]).

Apart from these core reports, subsequent studies have deepened our understanding on specific aspects of trade in counterfeit goods. These include Trade in Counterfeit Goods and Free Trade Zones: Evidence from Recent Trends (OECD/EUIPO, 2018[4]); Why Do Countries Export Fakes? (OECD/EUIPO, 2018[5]); Misuse of Small Parcels for Trade in Counterfeit Goods (OECD/EUIPO, 2018[6]); Trade in Counterfeit Pharmaceutical Goods (OECD/EUIPO, 2020[7]) and Misuse of Containerized Maritime Transport in Counterfeit Trade (OCDE/EUIPO, 2021[8]).

Altogether, these reports provide robust evidence of the significant volume of trade counterfeiting and piracy. They also document the large extent of this threat to efficient business and the well-being of consumers worldwide and point to the damages it causes by reducing firms' revenues and undermining their incentives to innovate.

The existing studies triggered great policy attention on combating counterfeit and pirated trade. This has been paralleled by increased efforts by the private sector to raise awareness of this threat. However, the existing dataset is becoming dated, and this could hamper understanding of the recent trends linked to trade in counterfeit goods.

In addition, several recent developments could also affect the current state of the trade in counterfeits. This includes the boom in trade in small parcels, which has been boosted by the COVID-19 pandemic.

What is more, the lockdowns and border closures of the on-going sanitary crisis has created – and will continue to create – further impacts on the illicit trade in counterfeit goods. These impacts occur through several direct and indirect transmission channels, including such phenomena as shifting consumer demand, changing priorities in customs controls and re-shaping trade routes.

This report provides policymakers with updated information on the trade in counterfeit and pirated goods. It measures the scale of counterfeiting using of the methodology developed in the (OCDE, 2008[9]) report and updated in (OECD/EUIPO, 2016[1]). This methodology is used with a new set of world data on seizures of counterfeit and pirated goods, leading to a set of objectives and a robust illustration of economy- and industry-specific patterns in the trade of counterfeits.

The authors stress that the quantitative analysis predates the COVID-19 pandemic. It is clear the pandemic has largely reshaped both licit trade and the trade in counterfeit goods. While some initial effects on counterfeiting having already been observed, the longer-term impact is expected to emerge gradually. Given the fast pace of change, a precise quantitative analysis of this has not yet been possible. Nevertheless, discussions with law enforcement officials and industry representatives, along with monitoring ongoing law enforcement actions, have shown that the main impact thus far has been an accelerated transition to e-commerce, with a boom in offers of counterfeits online (OECD, 2020[10]); (UNICRI, 2020[11]).

This study largely draws on statistical data on counterfeiting and piracy, which due to their nature are largely incomplete and limited. Consequently, the quantitative results presented in this study illustrate only certain parts of counterfeiting and piracy. Despite this, the methodological apparatus was tailored to the available dataset to ensure the conclusions are clear and based on fact.

Scope of the study

Counterfeiting and piracy are terms used to describe a range of illicit activities related to the infringement of intellectual property rights (IPRs). Following the (OCDE, 2008[9]), (OECD/EUIPO, 2016[1]) and (OECD/EUIPO, 2019[3]) studies, this report refers to the definitions as described in the World Trade Organization (WTO) Agreement on Trade-Related Aspects of Intellectual Property Rights (TRIPS Agreement). Consequently, this report focuses primarily on the infringement of copyright, trademarks, design rights and patents. The term counterfeit used in this report refers to tangible goods that infringe trademarks, design rights or patents, and the term pirated describes tangible goods that infringe copyright.

Three relevant aspects should be kept in mind in this context:

- This wording is used for the purpose of this report only and does not constitute any definition outside its scope.
- This study does not include intangible infringements, such as online piracy or infringements of other IPRs.
- Substandard, adulterated or mislabelled products, for example pharmaceuticals, that do not violate a trademark, patent or design right, for example, and replacement automotive oil filters and head lamps that are made by firms other than the original equipment manufacturer (OEM) (provided the replacement parts do not violate a patent, trademark or design right) are beyond the scope of this study.

Trends in global trade prior to the COVID-19 pandemic

Markets for infringing products develop dynamically and have been affected by several economic developments over the past ten years. Some of these major patterns are likely to shape the overall economic background for the evolution of the trade in counterfeit goods.

Following a decrease from 2014 to 2016, world trade grew by almost 22% from 2016 to 2018 and then decreased 2.7% from 2018 to 2019.

Figure 1.1. World trade flows, merchandise trade

Annual value in USD million

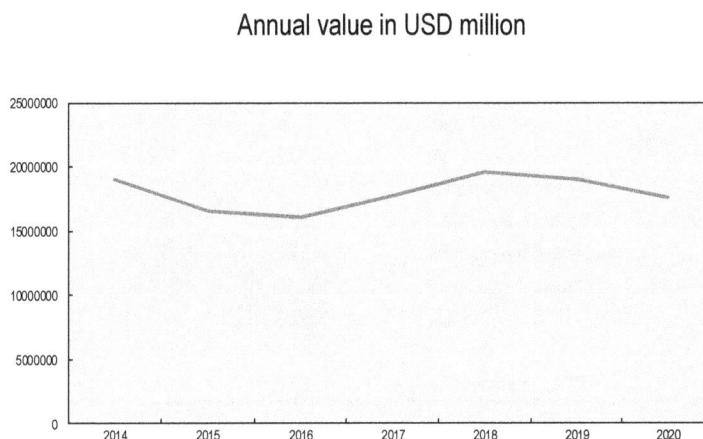

Source: WTO (2021), *Statistics on merchandise trade.*

Looking at world trade by sector, the increase in global trade was driven by fossil fuels and mining goods, with slower growth in both agricultural products and manufacturing. (Figure 1.2.).

Figure 1.2. Index of world trade by sector

Annual, 2016=100

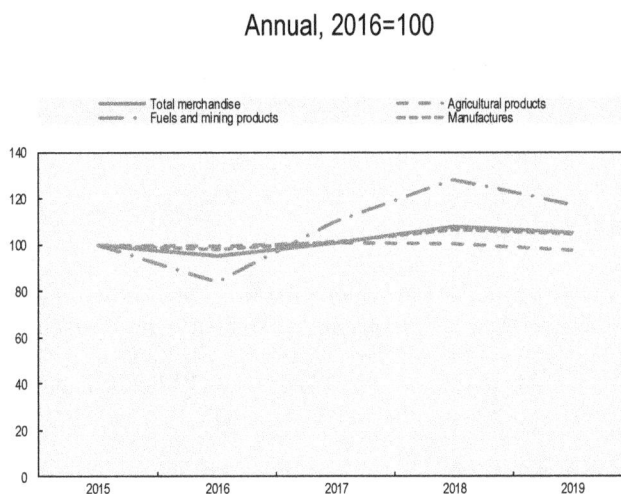

Source: WTO (2021), *Statistics on merchandise trade.*

The slow growth in commodity trade mostly halted in 2018. However, in 2019 the volumes of trade were still higher than in 2016 across all sectors that suffer from counterfeiting, for example, machinery, chemicals, food, textiles and office equipment.

Table 1.1. Index of world trade by main product category

Annual, 2016=100

Sector	2017	2018	2019
Agricultural products	108.95	113.99	112.68
Food	108.39	112.97	112.81
Fuels and mining products	128.17	159.95	151.19
Fuels	130.23	168.72	158.09
Manufacturing	108.79	117.86	115.57
Iron and steel	120.94	136.85	121.58
Chemicals	109.29	122.79	120.76
Pharmaceuticals	105.16	117.97	124.27
Machinery and transport equipment	109.69	118.12	115.40
Office and telecom equipment	113.65	123.38	118.83
Transport equipment	106.30	110.96	108.30
Textiles	105.06	111.21	108.77
Clothing	104.53	111.10	110.96
Total merchandise	110.58	121.85	118.51

Source: WTO (2021), *Statistics on merchandise trade*.

References

OCDE (2008), *The Economic Impact of Counterfeiting and Piracy*, Éditions OCDE, Paris, https://doi.org/10.1787/9789264045521-en. [9]

OCDE/EUIPO (2021), *Misuse of Containerized Maritime Shipping in the Global Trade of Counterfeits*, Éditions OCDE, Paris,, https://doi.org/10.1787/e39d8939-en. [8]

OECD (2021), *COVID-19 vaccine and the Threat of Illicit Trade, Chair's Summary Note*, https://www.oecd.org/gov/illicit-trade/summary-note-covid-19-vaccine-and-the-threat-of-illicit-trade.pdf. [12]

OECD (2020), *Illicit Trade in a Time of Crisis. Chair's Summary Note*, https://www.oecd.org/gov/illicit-trade/oecd-webinar-illicit-trade-time-crisis-23-april.pdf. [10]

OECD (2020), *Trade in Fake Medicines at the Time of the Covid-19 Pandemics. Chair's Summary Note*, https://www.oecd.org/gov/illicit-trade/oecd-fake-medicines-webinar-june-10-summary-note.pdf. [14]

OECD (2018), *Governance Frameworks to Counter Illicit Trade*, OECD Publishing, Paris,, https://doi.org/10.1787/9789264291652-en. [13]

OECD/EUIPO (2020), *Trade in Counterfeit Pharmaceutical Products*, Illicit Trade, OECD Publishing, Paris, https://dx.doi.org/10.1787/a7c7e054-en. [7]

OECD/EUIPO (2019), *Trends in Trade in Counterfeit and Pirated Goods*, OECD Publishing, Paris,, https://doi.org/10.1787/g2g9f533-en. [3]

OECD/EUIPO (2018), *Misuse of Small Parcels for Trade in Counterfeit Goods: Facts and Trends*, OECD Publishing, Paris, https://doi.org/10.1787/9789264307858-en. [6]

OECD/EUIPO (2018), *Trade in Counterfeit Goods and Free Trade Zones: Evidence from Recent Trends*, OECD Publishing, Paris/EUIPO, Alicante, https://doi.org/10.1787/9789264289550-en. [4]

OECD/EUIPO (2018), *Why Do Countries Export Fakes?: The Role of Governance Frameworks, Enforcement and Socio-economic Factors*, OECD Publishing, Paris/EUIPO, Alicante, https://doi.org/10.1787/9789264302464-en. [5]

OECD/EUIPO (2017), *Mapping the Real Routes of Trade in Fake Goods, Illicit Trade*, OECD Publishing, Paris, https://doi.org/10.1787/9789264278349-en. [2]

OECD/EUIPO (2016), *Trade in Counterfeit and Pirated Goods: Mapping the Economic Impact, Illicit Trade*, OECD Publishing, Paris, https://doi.org/10.1787/9789264252653-en. [1]

UNICRI (2020), *"Cyber-crime during the COVID-19 Pandemic"*, http://www.unicri.it/news/cyber-crime-during-covid-19-pandemic. [11]

Chapter 2. Updating the picture

Data

Following the approach taken in the (OCDE, 2008[9]) report and the (OECD/EUIPO, 2016[1]) and (OECD/EUIPO, 2019[3]) reports, the analysis in this report is based on international trade statistics and customs seizures of infringing products.

Trade data

The trade statistics are based on the United Nations (UN) Comtrade database (based on the value of merchandise assigned by customs officials, i.e. the landed customs value). With 171 reporting economies and 247 partner economies, the database covers the majority of world trade and is considered the most comprehensive trade database available. Products are registered based on the six-digit Harmonised System (HS) (an international commodity classification system, developed and maintained by the World Customs Organization [WCO]), meaning that the level of detail is high. Data used in this study are based on landed customs value. In most instances, this is the same as the transaction value appearing on accompanying invoices. Landed customs value includes the insurance and freight charges incurred when transporting goods from the economy of origin to the economy of importation.

Seizure data

Data on customs seizures originate from national customs administrations. This report relies on customs seizure data from the WCO, the European Commission's Directorate-General for Taxation and Customs Union (DG TAXUD) and from the United States Department of Homeland Security (DHS). The latter submitted seizure data from US Customs and Border Protection (CBP), the American customs agency, and from the US Immigration and Customs Enforcement (ICE).

In each year analysed (2017, 2018 and 2019), the total number of customs seizures of counterfeit and pirated goods worldwide consistently exceeded 130 000. Overall, the unified database on customs seizures of IP-infringing goods includes almost 465 000 observations, as compared to the 428 000 recorded from 2011-13 (OECD/EUIPO, 2016[1]).

A detailed analysis of these data revealed a set of limitations. Some of them are to do with discrepancies between the datasets, others product classification levels or outliers in terms of seized goods or provenance economies. All limitations were thoroughly discussed in the (OECD/EUIPO, 2016[1]) and (OECD/EUIPO, 2019[3]) reports, and a methodological way forward was proposed for each limitation. This report also relies on the same methodology presented and discussed in the 2016 study, and it employs the same solutions to the seizure-data limitations.

Methodological and statistical aspects: The GTRIC methodology

The GTRIC (General Trade-Related Index of Counterfeiting) methodology employed in this report draws on the one used in the (OECD/EUIPO, 2016[1]) study. This methodology in turn was based on the one used in the (OCDE, 2008[9]). A brief overview of these key components is presented below, and more details can be found in the (OECD/EUIPO, 2016[1]) report. Detailed, technical and methodological notes can be found in Annex A at the end of this report

Industry analysis (GTRIC-p)

The GTRIC-p (General Trade-Related Index of Counterfeiting for products) index represents the relative likelihood for products in one category to be counterfeit in comparison with another. It is done based on a customs data system that includes the 96 two-digit product modules included in the HS. In particular, if any of the reporting customs authorities registered a fake good in a given HS category, the whole category is treated as sensitive. Of course, within any category there may be considerable variation among products. The GTRIC-p index must therefore be seen as averages for the hundreds of goods covered by each HS chapter.

The GTRIC-p is compiled in two steps. In the first step, the seizure intensities in each product category are weighted by the respective share in total imports of these products of each reporting economy. This reflects the sensitivity of product infringements occurring in a particular product category relative to the intensity of imports of the products for each reporting economy. In the second step, these indices are transformed statistically to account for a number of known biases related to seizure techniques and propensities for which products in international trade are counterfeited and/or pirated.

Provenance economies (GTRIC-e)

The GTRIC-e (General Trade-Related Index of Counterfeiting for economies) index represents the relative likelihood for a given provenance economy to export fakes in comparison with other economies.

A provenance economy refers to where the production of infringing goods takes place, as well as economies that function as ports of transit through which infringing goods pass prior to reaching the economy of destination.

As with the GTRIC-p, the propensity for a given provenance economy is obtained by relating the weighted average of its seizure percentages to the respective share of total imports. The GTRIC-e is then determined along the same lines as the GTRIC-p and indicates the relative propensity of importing infringing goods from different provenance economies.

The trade in counterfeits as a whole

The GTRIC assigns the relative likelihood of there being counterfeit products in each product category and from each provenance economy.

The GTRIC index itself can be represented as a matrix table in which provenance economies are listed across the rows and in which the two-digit HS modules are listed in columns. Each element of the matrix, i.e. the value of GTRIC, denotes the relative propensity of a given provenance economy to export infringing products covered by a given HS module. These propensities can only be interpreted relative to each other; the GTRIC itself does not provide any information about the absolute magnitude of counterfeiting and piracy in world trade. Instead, the index should be considered as a tool to aid better appraisal of the problem of counterfeit and pirated trade. To go one step further and calculate the absolute value of counterfeit and pirated products in international trade, it is important to identify at least one probability of there being counterfeit and pirated products in a given product category from at least one provenance economy. This is established through structured interviews with industry experts and enforcement officials.

References

OCDE (2008), *The Economic Impact of Counterfeiting and Piracy*, Éditions OCDE, Paris, https://doi.org/10.1787/9789264045521-en. [9]

OCDE/EUIPO (2021), *Misuse of Containerized Maritime Shipping in the Global Trade of Counterfeits*, Éditions OCDE, Paris,, https://doi.org/10.1787/e39d8939-en. [8]

OECD (2021), *COVID-19 vaccine and the Threat of Illicit Trade, Chair's Summary Note*, https://www.oecd.org/gov/illicit-trade/summary-note-covid-19-vaccine-and-the-threat-of-illicit-trade.pdf. [12]

OECD (2020), *Illicit Trade in a Time of Crisis. Chair's Summary Note*, https://www.oecd.org/gov/illicit-trade/oecd-webinar-illicit-trade-time-crisis-23-april.pdf. [10]

OECD (2020), *Trade in Fake Medicines at the Time of the Covid-19 Pandemics. Chair's Summary Note*, https://www.oecd.org/gov/illicit-trade/oecd-fake-medicines-webinar-june-10-summary-note.pdf. [14]

OECD (2018), *Governance Frameworks to Counter Illicit Trade*, OECD Publishing, Paris,, https://doi.org/10.1787/9789264291652-en. [13]

OECD/EUIPO (2020), *Trade in Counterfeit Pharmaceutical Products*, Illicit Trade, OECD Publishing, Paris, https://dx.doi.org/10.1787/a7c7e054-en. [7]

OECD/EUIPO (2019), *Trends in Trade in Counterfeit and Pirated Goods*, OECD Publishing, Paris,, https://doi.org/10.1787/g2g9f533-en. [3]

OECD/EUIPO (2018), *Misuse of Small Parcels for Trade in Counterfeit Goods: Facts and Trends*, OECD Publishing, Paris, https://doi.org/10.1787/9789264307858-en. [6]

OECD/EUIPO (2018), *Trade in Counterfeit Goods and Free Trade Zones: Evidence from Recent Trends*, OECD Publishing, Paris/EUIPO, Alicante, https://doi.org/10.1787/9789264289550-en. [4]

OECD/EUIPO (2018), *Why Do Countries Export Fakes?: The Role of Governance Frameworks, Enforcement and Socio-economic Factors*, OECD Publishing, Paris/EUIPO, Alicante, https://doi.org/10.1787/9789264302464-en. [5]

OECD/EUIPO (2017), *Mapping the Real Routes of Trade in Fake Goods, Illicit Trade*, OECD Publishing, Paris, https://doi.org/10.1787/9789264278349-en. [2]

OECD/EUIPO (2016), *Trade in Counterfeit and Pirated Goods: Mapping the Economic Impact, Illicit Trade*, OECD Publishing, Paris, https://doi.org/10.1787/9789264252653-en. [1]

UNICRI (2020), *"Cyber-crime during the COVID-19 Pandemic"*, http://www.unicri.it/news/cyber-crime-during-covid-19-pandemic. [11]

Chapter 3. The trade in fakes: A first glance

This chapter presents a set of initial snapshots of the trade in fakes based on raw customs-seizure data.

Overview of seizures of counterfeit goods

In each analysed year (2017, 2018 and 2019), the total number of customs seizures of counterfeit and pirated goods worldwide consistently exceeded 130 000. Overall, the unified database on customs seizures of IP-infringing goods includes almost half million observations. These data provide a wealth of information about provenance economies, the industry scope of the trade in counterfeits and the economies where rights holders whose IP rights are infringed are registered.

In most cases, the data do not allow distinguishing whether seized goods come from the original point of manufacturing or from a transit point. Therefore, as detailed in the (OECD/EUIPO, 2016[1]) report, the term provenance economies is employed. This term refers to economies where the actual production of infringing goods is taking place and economies that function as ports of transit through which infringing goods pass.

Provenance economies

Any economy can be the provenance of counterfeit and pirated trade, and the scope of these provenance economies is very broad. A descriptive analysis of the unified dataset of customs seizures identified 180 provenance economies of counterfeit and pirated products between 2017 and 2019, as compared to 184 from 2014 to 2016 and 173 from 2011 to 2013.

While the scope of provenance economies is broad, the raw seizures statistics show that interceptions originate from a relatively concentrated set of provenance economies. In other words, some economies tend to dominate the global trade in counterfeit and pirated goods. The highest number of counterfeit shipments seized is in East Asia, with China and Hong Kong (China) at the top of the ranking (Figure 3.1).

Figure 3.1. Top provenance economies of counterfeit and pirated goods in terms of customs seizures, 2017-19

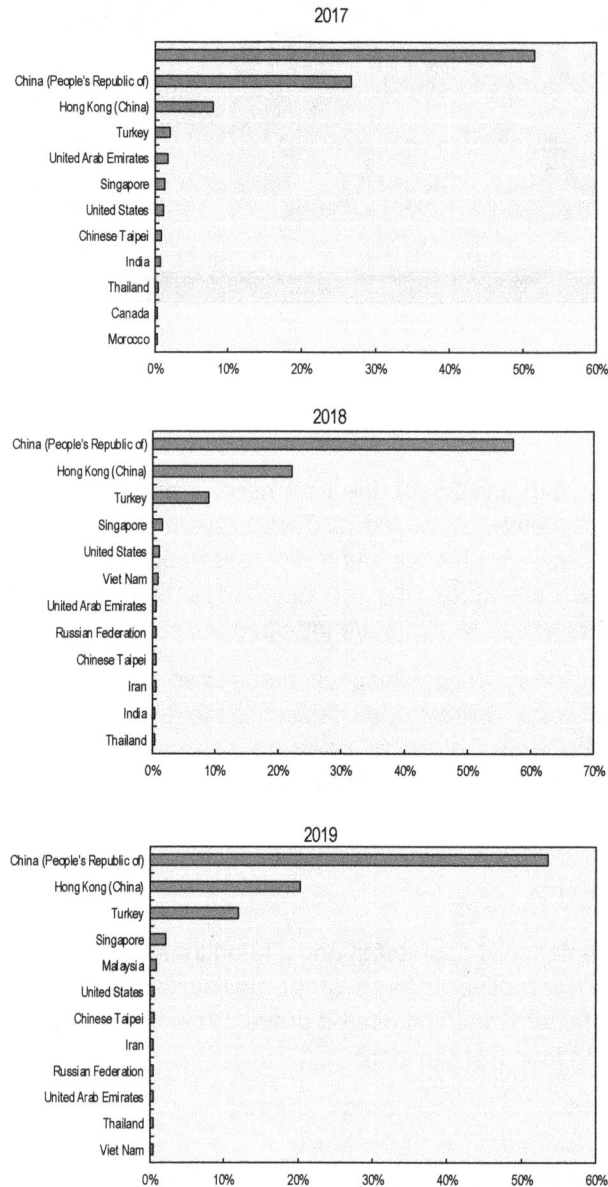

Source: OECD/EUIPO database.

China and Hong Kong (China) dominated the global trade in counterfeit goods in both 2016 and 2019 (Figure 3.2), with the latter's percentage decreasing when compared to 2016. The presence of Turkey among the top provenance economies of counterfeit goods increased over this period: its share of global seizures tripled between 2016 and 2019, rising from 4% to 12%.

Figure 3.2. Differences in provenance economies in counterfeit and pirated trade, 2017-19

Share of global customs seizures of IP-infringing goods

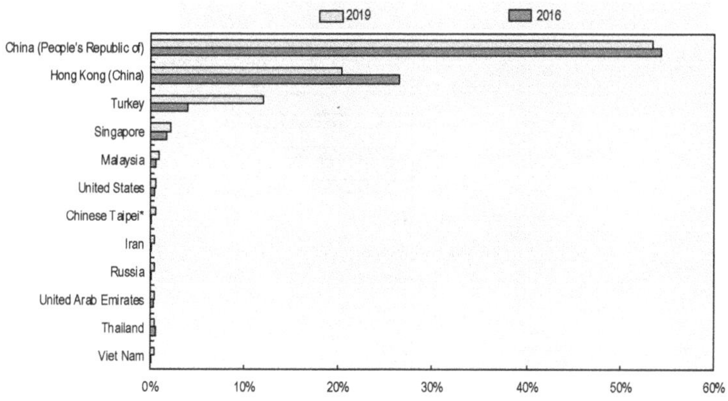

Source: OECD/EUIPO database.

Product categories

The unique dataset of customs seizures is also used to analyse the types of products subject to counterfeiting. It shows that a wide range of products is counterfeited and pirated. Indeed, the statistics on customs seizures reveal that between 2017 and 2019, customs detected articles in violation of intellectual property rights in 83 of the 96 HS chapters. This means that almost any kind of product is targeted by counterfeiters and may suffer from IP infringement.

However, statistics on customs seizures also indicate that interceptions of fake goods are not uniform, and some product categories seem to be reported more often by customs. The most frequently seized products were footwear, clothing, leather goods, and electrical machinery and electronic equipment (Figure 3.3)

Figure 3.3. Top product categories of counterfeit and pirated goods, 2017-19

(In terms of global customs seizures)

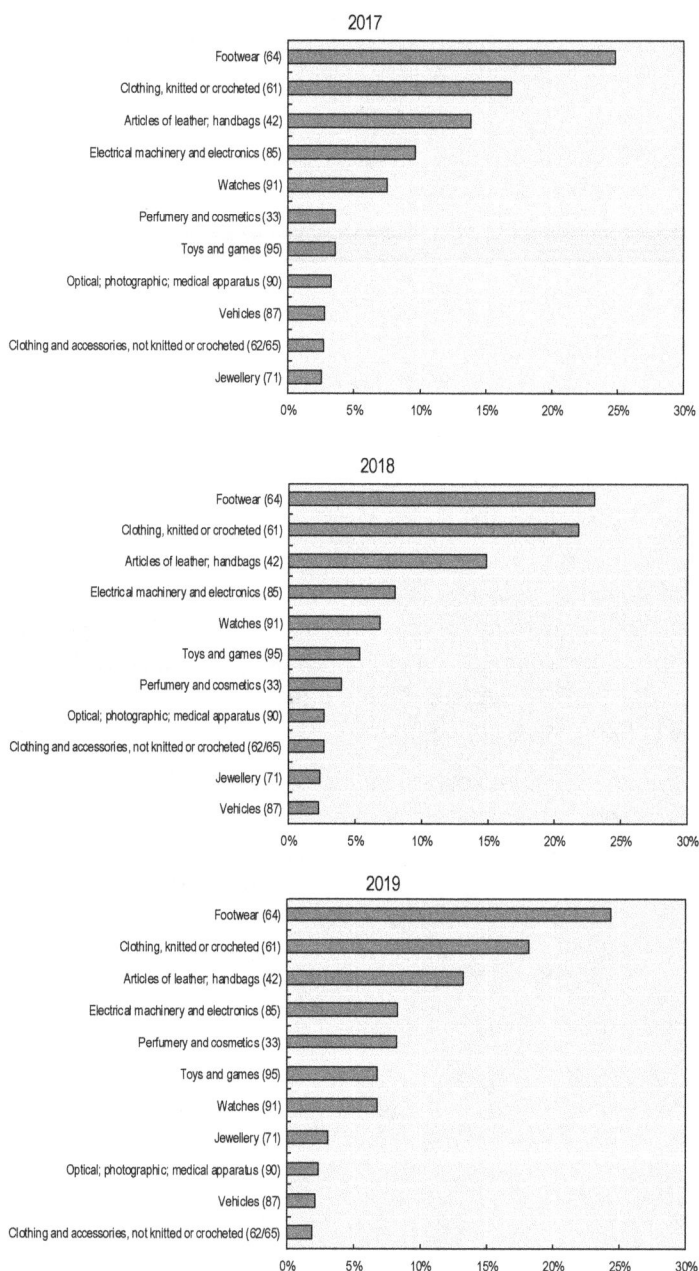

2017

Category	
Footwear (64)	~25%
Clothing, knitted or crocheted (61)	~17%
Articles of leather; handbags (42)	~14%
Electrical machinery and electronics (85)	~9%
Watches (91)	~7%
Perfumery and cosmetics (33)	~4%
Toys and games (95)	~4%
Optical; photographic; medical apparatus (90)	~3%
Vehicles (87)	~3%
Clothing and accessories, not knitted or crocheted (62/65)	~3%
Jewellery (71)	~2%

2018

Category	
Footwear (64)	~23%
Clothing, knitted or crocheted (61)	~22%
Articles of leather; handbags (42)	~15%
Electrical machinery and electronics (85)	~8%
Watches (91)	~7%
Toys and games (95)	~5%
Perfumery and cosmetics (33)	~4%
Optical; photographic; medical apparatus (90)	~3%
Clothing and accessories, not knitted or crocheted (62/65)	~3%
Jewellery (71)	~2%
Vehicles (87)	~2%

2019

Category	
Footwear (64)	~24%
Clothing, knitted or crocheted (61)	~18%
Articles of leather; handbags (42)	~13%
Electrical machinery and electronics (85)	~8%
Perfumery and cosmetics (33)	~8%
Toys and games (95)	~7%
Watches (91)	~7%
Jewellery (71)	~3%
Optical; photographic; medical apparatus (90)	~2%
Vehicles (87)	~2%
Clothing and accessories, not knitted or crocheted (62/65)	~2%

Note: Figures in parentheses refer to the HS Code.
Source: OECD/EUIPO database.

Figure 3.4 indicates the top eight product categories most subject to counterfeiting and piracy remained the same from 2011 to 2019. However, some changes can be noted. In 2019, fake electrical machinery and electronics were less frequently seized by customs than in 2016, while counterfeit toys, games, perfumery and cosmetics were more often reported.

Figure 3.4. Differences in product categories most subject to counterfeiting and piracy, 2016 and 2019

In terms of share of global customs seizures

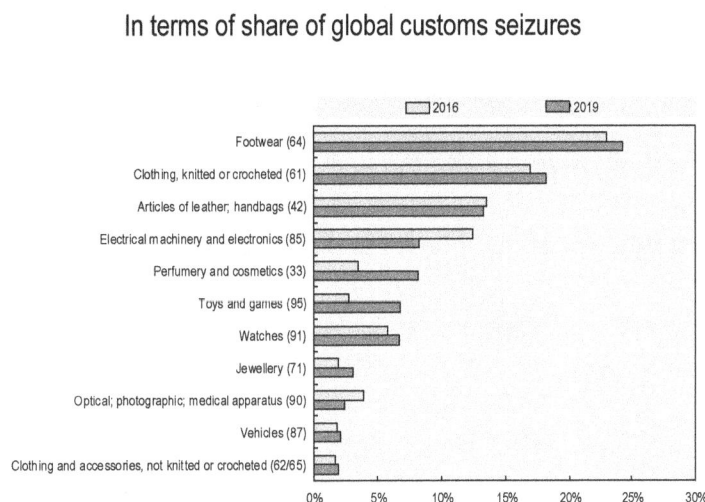

Note: Figure in parenthesis refer to the HS Code.
Source: OECD/EUIPO database.

As long as a given product is protected with a trademark, patent, design right or copyright, it is likely that it is counterfeited and pirated. The scope of counterfeiting and piracy is broad and covers almost all products that are protected by the four IP rights mentioned above. Existing statistics report on seizures of such wide-ranging counterfeit products (i.e. trademark infringing) as fresh strawberries, breathing apparatuses and artificial grass, just as in 2016 examples of counterfeit goods included coconut oil, guitars and construction materials. This proof that counterfeiters use aggressive strategies, looking for all kinds of opportunities to make a profit.

The descriptive analysis of the seizures database shows a large number of seized IP-infringing packaging and labels. For the 2019 period, the unified dataset includes almost six thousand customs seizures of counterfeit labels, a 20% increase on 2016. This re-confirms findings about the domestic assembly of counterfeit and pirated products from imported materials, formulated in a study by OHIM-Europol (2015).

If the counterfeit products most frequently seized are common products, it should be noted that many counterfeit products represent a real threat for consumer health and safety as well as the environment. These include fake foodstuffs, toys, cosmetics and chemicals. Counterfeit chemical products, such as fertilizers or pesticides, may raise environmental issues.

Last but not least, the counterfeiting of pharmaceuticals products is a reality. Even though they are not the most infringed products, their trade is a real threat to public health and was documented by the OECD and EUIPO in (OECD/EUIPO, 2020[7]). The findings show that both common medicines as well as more complex drugs (i.e. for cancer or heart disease) are counterfeited.

These challenges have become even greater with the COVID-19 pandemic, which has created new opportunities for profits for criminal networks. Supply chains broken by border closures, a strong demand for medicines, protective equipment and tests, and the limited capacity of law enforcement officials all shape the illicit trade in fake pharmaceuticals. Criminals are clearly taking advantage of the global pandemic, and enforcement authorities are reporting a sharp increase in seizures of fake and substandard medicines, test kits and personal protective equipment (PPE), as well as other medical products. In addition, the first instances of counterfeit COVID-19 vaccine have been reported, posing a vital threat to vaccination programmes.

Conveyance methods and extent of seizures

Descriptive statistics on customs seizures highlight that the postal service was the most popular way of shipping counterfeit and pirated products (Figure 3.5) in terms on frequency of seizures. Between 2017 and 2019, postal shipment was the transport mode of 64% of global seizures, and 13% of seizures concerned express courier. This indicates that the use of the postal and express services dominates in terms of number of seizures, accounting for 77% of global seizures, up from 69% of global seizures from 2014 to 2016. Postal shipments were followed by air, at 14% of global seizures, and sea, at 5%.

Figure 3.5. Conveyance methods for counterfeit and pirated products, 2017-19

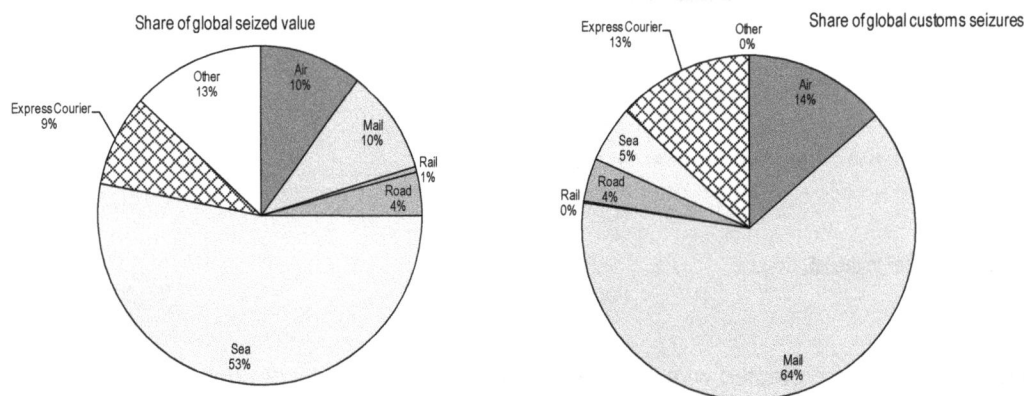

Source: OECD/EUIPO data

The unique dataset on customs seizures also enables to analyse quantities of seized counterfeit and pirated goods (Figure 3.6), indicating the size of seized shipments tends to be small. Indeed, shipments containing less than 10 items accounted for 61% of the total number of shipments. During the previous period, small shipments (i.e. less than 10 items) were also the most popular conveyance method for counterfeit and pirated goods, representing 65% of the total number of shipments. This is a key trend in the trade in fake goods and was highlighted in the (OECD/EUIPO, 2018[6]) report on small parcels.

The sizes of seized shipments tend to be small: shipments with fewer than 10 items accounted for about two thirds of the total number of shipments on average, against 85% and 43% for the 2014-16 and 2011-13 periods, respectively (Figure 3.6). This matches the finding that in terms of the number of seizures small parcels usually containing a few items remain the most popular conveyance method for counterfeit and pirated products.

Figure 3.6. Size of seized shipments, 2017-19

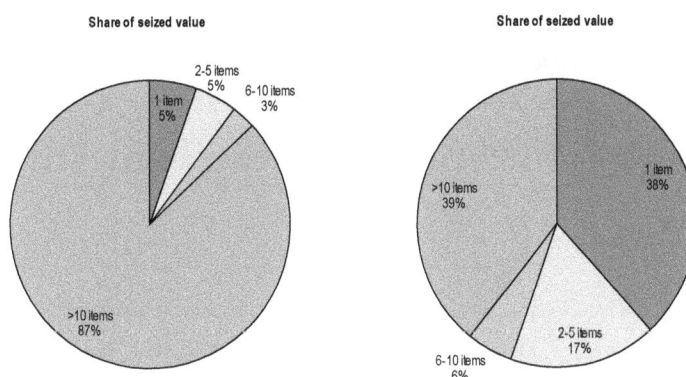

Source : OECD/EUIPO database

References

OCDE (2008), *The Economic Impact of Counterfeiting and Piracy*, Éditions OCDE, Paris, https://doi.org/10.1787/9789264045521-en. [9]

OCDE/EUIPO (2021), *Misuse of Containerized Maritime Shipping in the Global Trade of Counterfeits*, Éditions OCDE, Paris,, https://doi.org/10.1787/e39d8939-en. [8]

OECD (2021), *COVID-19 vaccine and the Threat of Illicit Trade, Chair's Summary Note*, https://www.oecd.org/gov/illicit-trade/summary-note-covid-19-vaccine-and-the-threat-of-illicit-trade.pdf. [12]

OECD (2020), *Illicit Trade in a Time of Crisis. Chair's Summary Note*, https://www.oecd.org/gov/illicit-trade/oecd-webinar-illicit-trade-time-crisis-23-april.pdf. [10]

OECD (2020), *Trade in Fake Medicines at the Time of the Covid-19 Pandemics. Chair's Summary Note*, https://www.oecd.org/gov/illicit-trade/oecd-fake-medicines-webinar-june-10-summary-note.pdf. [14]

OECD (2018), *Governance Frameworks to Counter Illicit Trade*, OECD Publishing, Paris,, https://doi.org/10.1787/9789264291652-en. [13]

OECD/EUIPO (2020), *Trade in Counterfeit Pharmaceutical Products*, Illicit Trade, OECD Publishing, Paris, https://dx.doi.org/10.1787/a7c7e054-en. [7]

OECD/EUIPO (2019), *Trends in Trade in Counterfeit and Pirated Goods*, OECD Publishing, Paris,, https://doi.org/10.1787/g2g9f533-en. [3]

OECD/EUIPO (2018), *Misuse of Small Parcels for Trade in Counterfeit Goods: Facts and Trends*, OECD Publishing, Paris, https://doi.org/10.1787/9789264307858-en. [6]

OECD/EUIPO (2018), *Trade in Counterfeit Goods and Free Trade Zones: Evidence from Recent Trends*, OECD Publishing, Paris/EUIPO, Alicante, https://doi.org/10.1787/9789264289550-en. [4]

OECD/EUIPO (2018), *Why Do Countries Export Fakes?: The Role of Governance Frameworks, Enforcement and Socio-economic Factors*, OECD Publishing, Paris/EUIPO, Alicante, https://doi.org/10.1787/9789264302464-en. [5]

OECD/EUIPO (2017), *Mapping the Real Routes of Trade in Fake Goods, Illicit Trade*, OECD Publishing, Paris, https://doi.org/10.1787/9789264278349-en. [2]

OECD/EUIPO (2016), *Trade in Counterfeit and Pirated Goods: Mapping the Economic Impact, Illicit Trade*, OECD Publishing, Paris, https://doi.org/10.1787/9789264252653-en. [1]

UNICRI (2020), *"Cyber-crime during the COVID-19 Pandemic"*, http://www.unicri.it/news/cyber-crime-during-covid-19-pandemic. [11]

Chapter 4. The trade in fakes: The current picture

The raw seizure data presented in the previous chapter do not take into account the general economic context, nevertheless they can be used as input for further statistical analysis. This is presented in the current chapter that summarizes the main results of the GTRIC analysis and our subsequent understanding of the trade in counterfeit and pirated goods. There are two areas in this analysis: the identification of key economies of provenance (i.e. the GTRIC-e) and the industry scope of the trade in counterfeit and pirated goods (i.e. the GTRIC-p).

Provenance economies

Figure 4.1 indicates that many economies are part of the list of exporters of counterfeit products. However, it also indicates that most counterfeit products originated from a small group of economies. From 2017-19, these economies were China, Hong Kong (China), Turkey, Singapore and the United Arab Emirates (UAE). On average 90% of global seizures came from these five countries during this period.

Figure 4.1. Top 25 provenance economies for counterfeit and pirated goods, 2017-19

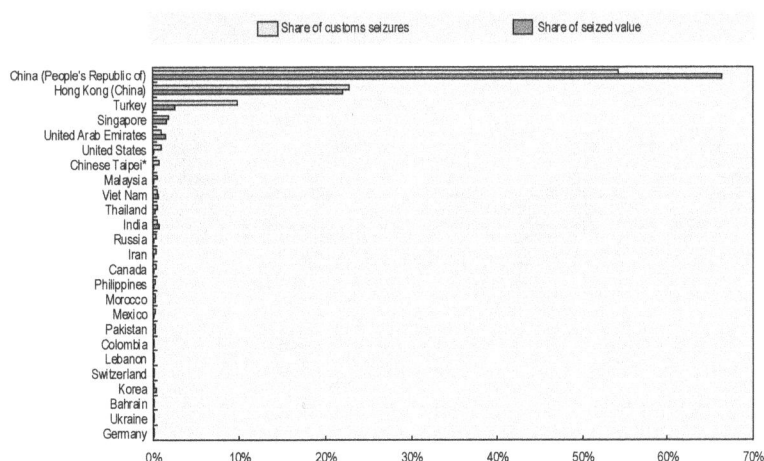

Source: OECD/EUIPO database.

Descriptive statistics on provenance economies of counterfeit and pirated products illustrate the significance of counterfeiting and piracy in international trade. Of course, many of the economies identified as provenance economies are also important actors in world trade in general. The economy-specific index, based on the methodology presented in Chapter 2 and Annex A, takes this into account and provides a more precise analysis. Specifically, it considers both: the share of seizures and the trade flows of the analysed economy. Hence, the index (called GTRIC-e) captures the relative propensity of importing counterfeits from different provenance economies.

Table 4.1 shows the top provenance economies in terms of their propensity to export counterfeit products from 2017-19. During this period, Hong Kong (China), the Syrian Arab Republic, China and Turkey were at the top of the ranking. This means that these economies have a high GTRIC-e score and are either reported as a provenance of high values of counterfeit and pirated products in absolute terms (e.g. USD) or their share of counterfeit and pirated goods is high.

Table 4.1. Top 25 provenance economies in terms of their propensity to export counterfeit products

GTRIC-e, average 2017-19

Provenance economy	GTRIC-e
Hong Kong (China)	1
Syrian Arab Republic	0.998
China (People's Republic of)	0.998
Turkey	0.996
Dominican Republic	0.984
Pakistan	0.955
Georgia	0.933
Lebanon	0.872
Senegal	0.831
Afghanistan	0.761
Singapore	0.758
Benin	0.727
UAE	0.720
Morocco	0.694
Cambodia	0.684
Bangladesh	0.661
Curaçao	0.635
Panama	0.616
Tokelau	0.580
Albania	0.577
Serbia	0.545
Paraguay	0.451
India	0.447
Lao People's Democratic Republic	0.441

Note: High GTRIC-e is a weighted value of two sub-components: the value of exports of counterfeit and pirated products from that economy in absolute terms and the share of trade in counterfeit and pirated products from that economy.

Hong Kong and China were already at the top of the provenance economies from 2014-16, with the highest propensity to export counterfeit products. The UAE and Morocco have moved down the ranking from 2017-19, while the Dominican Republic and Singapore have moved up.

The Syrian Arab Republic moved into second position from 16th from 2014-16, with a GTRIC-e of 0.561. Further analysis from additional data needs to be carried out to determine whether the Syrian Arab Republic is a seasonal or a continuous point of transfer for the world trade in fakes. Changes in transit points may come from the application of effective anti-counterfeiting policies by enforcement authorities or due to other factors, such as the evolution of trades flow in general or the emergence of other, such as more convenient routes of trade in fakes. In addition, some economies on the list, such as Syria or Venezuela, are rather unstable. It shows that such conditions do not deter criminals that operate illicit trade network, who in fact benefit from these political uncertainties

As mentioned above, it is important to note that the GTRIC-e presents the key provenance economies in the trade of counterfeits; they may be economies either where the actual production of infringing goods is taking place or economies where infringing goods transit. Further analysis in relevant industries is carried out in the subchapter below to determine whether an economy is a producer of fake goods or a place of transit.

Impacted industries

As discussed in Chapter 3, the scope of goods that are sensitive to infringement is broad and has broadened (88 of the 96 HS chapters are affected by counterfeiting and piracy, i.e. 92% for the 2017-19 period versus 80% for the 2011-13 period). However, the intensity of counterfeiting and piracy differs greatly for different types of goods and hence across HS categories. This is illustrated in Figure 4.2 below, which indicates that between 2017 and 2019, interceptions were concentrated in a relatively limited number of chapters.

As can be seen in Figure 4.2, the scope of goods that are subject to infringement is broad. However, the intensity of counterfeiting and piracy differs significantly from one product category to another. Indeed, from 2017 to 2019 interceptions of counterfeit products remained concentrated in a relatively limited number of HS categories.

Figure 4.2. Top 20 product categories counterfeit and pirated, 2017-19

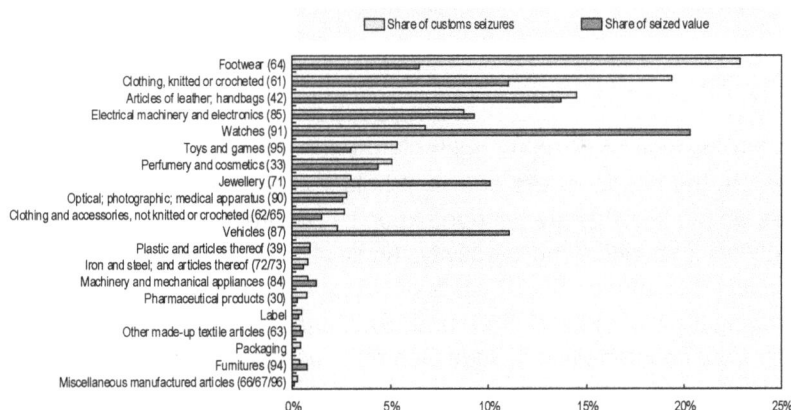

Source: OECD/EUIPO database.

From 2017 to 2019 the top five of industries targeted by counterfeiters remained exactly the same from 2014 to 2016. Perfumery and cosmetics, articles of leather, clothing, footwear and watches were again the industries with the highest propensity to be subject to counterfeiting.

However, the list of the top 20 industries that are targeted by counterfeiters changed slightly between 2011 to 2013 and 2014 to 2016. In the former period, the top three included watches, leather goods and headgear. In the latter perfumery and cosmetics, toys and clothing, and knitted or crocheted clothing were targeted.

Table 4.2. Top 20 industries targeted by counterfeiters, 2017-19

GTRIC-p, average

Harmonised System Code (HS Code)	GTRIC-p
Perfumery and cosmetics (33)	1.000
Articles of leather; handbags (42)	1.000
Clothing, knitted or crocheted (61)	1.000
Footwear (64)	1.000
Watches (91)	1.000
Toys and games (95)	1.000
Jewellery (71)	1.000
Tobacco (24)	0.997
Other made-up textile articles (63)	0.858
Arms and ammunition (93)	0.820
Clothing and accessories, not knitted or crocheted (62/65)	0.787
Musical instruments (92)	0.656
Knitted or crocheted fabrics (60)	0.633
Optical; photographic; medical apparatus (90)	0.596
Electrical machinery and electronics (85)	0.530
Furniture (94)	0.503
Miscellaneous articles of base metal (83)	0.373
Miscellaneous manufactured articles (66/67/96)	0.313
Printed articles (49)	0.273

Impacted economies

This section studies the location of IP rights holders that suffer from counterfeiting and piracy. Location refers to the place where the headquarters of a right holder is registered. As in previous years, the vast majority of companies whose IP rights are infringed upon by counterfeiters are located in OECD countries, whose economies rely on innovation and creativity. As illustrated in Figure 4.3, almost 39% of customs seizures refer to products that infringe the IP rights of US rights holders. The United States is followed by France (18%), Germany (16%), Italy (9.8%) and Switzerland (4%). Other OECD countries whose companies also suffer from counterfeiting include Denmark, Japan, Korea, Spain, Ireland and Sweden.

Remarkably, right holders in China and Hong Kong (China) also suffer from counterfeiting, as China and Hong Kong (China) rank 15th and 20th respectively in the list of economies most impacted by global counterfeiting and piracy. This phenomenon is interesting as these regions are also the top provenance economies for counterfeited and pirated products. This also indicates the strong threat that counterfeiting and piracy poses in undermining innovation within Chinese companies, since many of these companies rely on knowledge-based capital and IP rights in their business strategies.

Figure 4.3. Top economies of origin of right holders whose IP rights are infringed, 2017-19

In terms of number of customs seizures

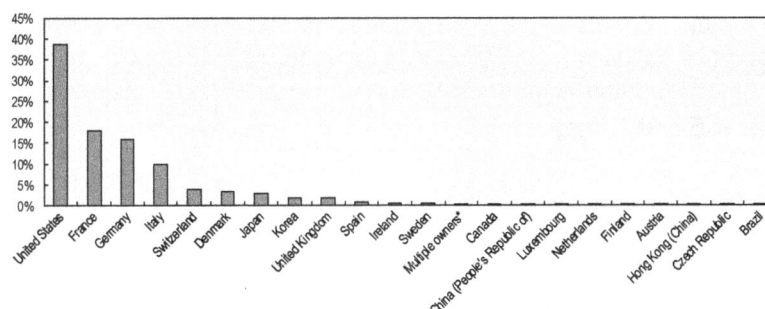

Source: OECD/EUIPO database.

Mapping real routes for trade in fakes: industry cases

Parties that trade in counterfeit and pirated products tend to ship infringing products via complex trade routes in order to cover their tracks. These complex routes are a formidable obstacle for enforcement authorities. Mapping the trade routes for fake goods is therefore essential in developing effective policies to counter this threat.

Precise information about the economy of origin is essential for efficient enforcement. Complex trade routes become a formidable obstacle for enforcement authorities, as the economy of origin is concealed through the various transit points. Consequently, a mapping of trade routes in fake goods is essential for developing effective policies to counter these illicit activities. In response to this problem, we decided to chart the routes used in the trade of fakes to determine the main producers and identify the key transit points.

Determining the main producer economies of fakes and the key transit points requires statistical data on the seizures of counterfeit and pirated goods, complemented with international trade statistics and data on industrial activity (a detailed description of these data and the related limitations is presented in Annex A).

The methodology is used to determine first the top economies of provenance for counterfeit goods in each product category. However, it does not distinguish whether these economies are producers or transit points of fake goods in the category. Then, it applies a filter to distinguish the producing economies from the key potential transit points for each analysed industry in each economy. Filters are based on data that gauge economies' propensities to produce and to re-export these goods.

Logically, if an economy is not a significant producer of a fake good and at the same time is a large re-exporter of this good in legitimate trade, then it is likely to be a transit point. Similarly, economies that are identified as provenance economies that are significant producers of a given good but are insignificant re-exporters are likely to be producers of these fake products.

These filters are well grounded in the economic trade literature and are used to assess the specialisation and complexity of a given economy (Hidalgo and Hausmann, 2009 and 2011).

Trade routes for fake perfumery and cosmetics

Provenance and destination economies

According to the global customs seizure data, China was by far the largest provenance economy of counterfeit perfumery and cosmetics between 2017 and 2019. Indeed, China was the origin of 78% of the total seized value of worldwide counterfeit perfumery and cosmetics (Figure 4.4.). It was followed by India, Hong Kong (China), the UAE and Turkey.

Figure 4.4. Top provenance economies for counterfeit perfumery and cosmetics, 2017-19

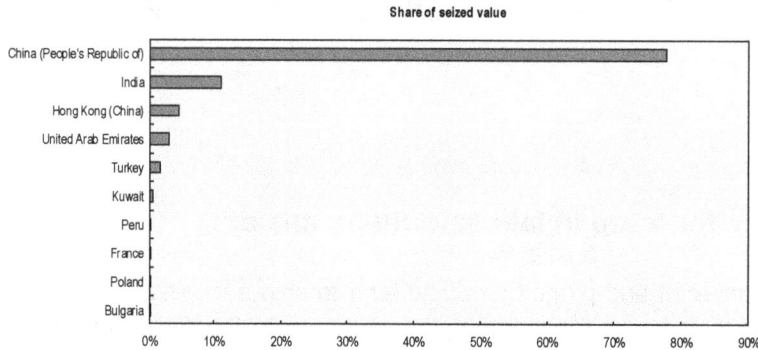

Source: OECD/EUIPO database.

The GTRIC-e index for the perfumery and cosmetics industry compares the customs seizures intensities of infringing perfumes and cosmetics with genuine trade intensities for each provenance economy. This confirms that China, Hong Kong (China) and India are the economies most likely to be the source of fake perfumes and cosmetics (Table 4.3). The GTRIC index shows that Kuwait, the UAE and Turkey are also part of the economies most likely to export fake perfumes and cosmetics. The list of top provenance economies for counterfeit perfumes and cosmetics imported into the EU is quite comparable to the one for world imports (Table 4.4).

Table 4.3. Relative likelihood of an economy to be a source of fake perfumery and cosmetics

GTRIC-e world for perfumes and cosmetics, average 2017-19

provenance	GTRIC-e
Hong Kong (China)	1
China (People's Republic of)	1
India	1
Kuwait	0.971
UAE	0.959
Turkey	0.935
Lebanon	0.699
Panama	0.618
Venezuela	0.502
Jordan	0.501
Nigeria	0.483
Bahrain	0.381
Bulgaria	0.341
Ethiopia	0.333

Note: A high score on the GTRIC index means there is a greater likelihood the economy is a source of counterfeit goods.

Table 4.4. Relative likelihood of an economy to be a source of fake perfumery and cosmetics imported into the EU

GTRIC-e for perfumes and cosmetics to the EU, average 2017-19

provenance	GTRIC-e
China (People's Republic of)	1
Hong Kong (China)	1
Venezuela	1
UAE	1
Turkey	0.999
Singapore	0.867
Malaysia	0.798
Belarus	0.745
Saudi Arabia	0.667
Ukraine	0.629
Bulgaria	0.628
Kuwait	0.628
Russia	0.506
Bahrain	0.333

Descriptive statistics on the most intensive routes presented in Figure 4.5. show that over the period 2017-19 the largest share of fake perfumery and cosmetics exported to the US and the EU came from China, India and Hong Kong (China).

Figure 4.5. Top provenance-destination economies for counterfeit perfume and cosmetics, 2017-19

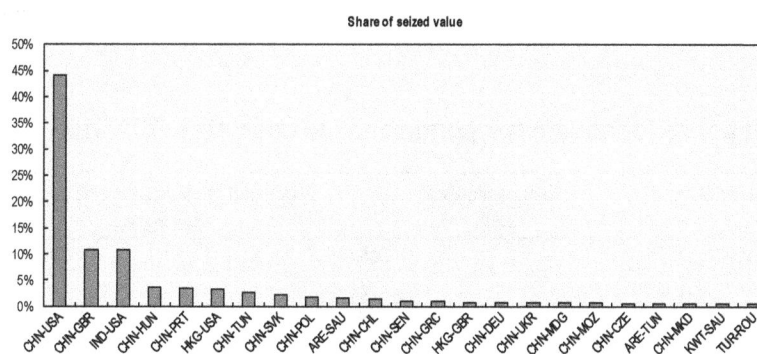

Source: OECD/EUIPO database.

Producers and transit points

Comparing the GTRIC-e indices with the Relative Comparative Advantage for Production (RCAP-e) and Relative Comparative Advantage for being a Transit Point (RCAT-e) indices indicates that China, Turkey, India and Singapore were the main producers of counterfeit perfumery and cosmetics (Table 4.5). While China exports fake perfumery and cosmetics across the world, the fakes exported by other producers were mainly destined to the US, the EU and countries in the Middle East.

Table 4.5. Producers of counterfeit perfumery and cosmetics, 2017-19

Producing economy	Destinations	Transport mode
China	EU	Mail - Air - Sea
	US	Mail - Air
	Saudi Arabia	Sea - Rail - Mail
	Kuwait	Sea
	Morocco	Sea
	Japan	Air - Mail
	African countries	Sea
	South American countries	Sea - Air
	Jordan	Sea - Mail
	Qatar	Sea
Turkey	EU	Road - Air - Mail
	Morocco	Sea
	Saudi Arabia	Air - Mail -Sea
	Qatar	Sea - Air
India	US	
	Saudi Arabia	Sea - Mail - Rail
	Qatar	Sea
	EU	Mail
Singapore	US	
	EU	Mail - Air
	Saudi Arabia	Sea

Comparing the GTRIC-e and RCAT-e indices allows identification of the transit points of counterfeit perfumes and cosmetics, indicating that Hong Kong (China) is an important hub for fake perfumes and cosmetics that are re-exported mainly to the EU and the US. The UAE and Kuwait are also used as transit points for re-exporting fake perfumery and cosmetics, particularly to the EU, the US and countries in the Middle East.

Table 4.6. Key transit points for counterfeit perfumery and cosmetics, 2017-19

Provenance economy	Transit point	Main destinations	Transport mode from transit point to destination
China UAE	Kuwait	Qatar	Sea - Air
		EU	Mail
		Saudi Arabia	Road - Mail
		UAB	Air
?	UAE	Saudi Arabia	Mail - Road - Sea
		Gulf countries (Kuwait, Oman and Bahrain)	Road - Sea
		EU	Sea - Air - Mail
		US	Sea
		Belarus	Sea
		Jordan	Sea - Road
?	Hong Kong (China)	US	Mail
		EU	Mail - Air - Sea
		Puerto Rico	Mail
		Japan	Air
		Saudi Arabia	Mail - Sea
		Senegal	Mail

Trade routes for fake leather articles and handbags

Provenance and destination economies

According to the OECD-EUIPO database on global customs seizures, China was by far the main provenance economy of fake leather articles and handbags between 2017 and 2019 (Figure 4.6.). China was the origin of 59% of the total seized value in this product category. It was followed by Hong Kong (China) (33%) and Turkey (5%).

Figure 4.6. Top provenance economies of counterfeit leather articles and handbags, 2017-19

Share of global seized value

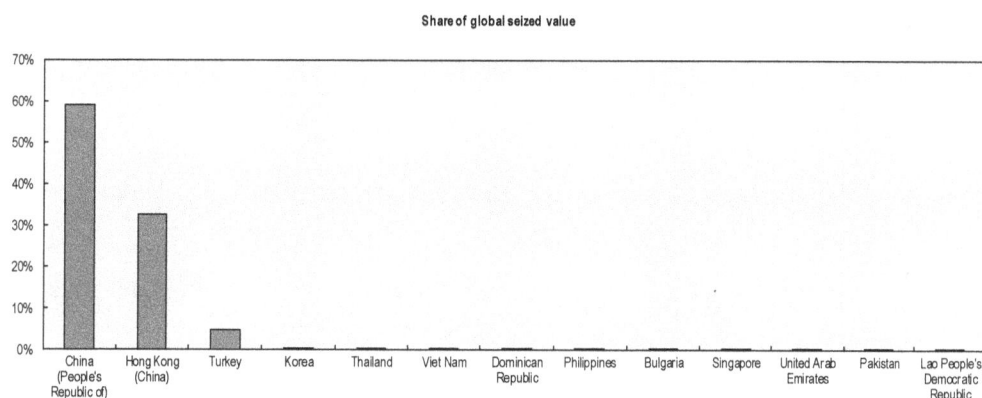

Source: OECD/EUIPO database.

The GTRIC-e indices compare the customs seizures intensities of infringing products with licit trade intensities for each provenance economy. The GTRIC-e indices for leather articles show that several economies are likely to be a source of counterfeit articles of leather. Compared to the 2011-13 period, there are many more economies associated with a high GTRIC score (i.e. 17 provenance economies display GTRIC-e scores higher than 0.9). According to the GTRIC-e index, the economies most likely to export fake articles of leather over the 2017-19 period were Afghanistan, Hong Kong (China), Iraq, Nigeria, Senegal, Venezuela, Cameroon, Lao and Jordan (Table 4.7). Among economies most likely to be a source of fake leather articles and handbags, there are several provenance economies that are more common sources of fakes, namely Hong Kong (China), Turkey, the UAE and China, as well as unusual provenance economies such as Afghanistan, Iraq, Iran, Nigeria, Senegal and Cameroon. These economies have a high GTRIC score because the value of seized fake articles of leather originating in these countries is high in relative terms (i.e. in terms of trade flows), while the seized value is limited in absolute terms (i.e. in terms of value in USD).

Table 4.7. Relative likelihood of an economy to be a source of counterfeit leather articles and handbags

GTRIC-e world for leather articles and handbags; average 2017-19

Provenance	GTRIC-e
Afghanistan	1
Hong Kong (China)	1
Iraq	1
Nigeria	1
Senegal	1
Venezuela	1
Cameroon	1
Lao People's Democratic Republic	1
Jordan	1
Bahrain	0.999
Turkey	0.999
Egypt	0.998
Iran	0.981
Kenya	0.936
Dominican Republic	0.929
UAE	0.918
Russia	0.912
Ecuador	0.844
China (People's Republic of)	0.742
Saudi Arabia	0.731
Colombia	0.696
Lebanon	0.688
Democratic Republic of the Congo	0.667
British Virgin Islands	0.667
Azerbaijan	0.657

The list of economies most likely to export fake leather goods to the EU is comparable to the one for worldwide exports of fake articles of leather. However, it should be noted that Singapore exports more fake leather goods to the EU than worldwide, and that Morocco and countries that are geographically close to the EU, such as Albania, Russia or Azerbaijan, also export fake articles of leather.

Table 4.8. Relative likelihood of an economy to be a source of counterfeit leather articles and handbags imported to the EU

GTRIC-e EU for leather articles and handbags; average 2017-19

provenance	GTRIC-e
Egypt	1
Iran	1
Nigeria	1
Russia	1
Senegal	1
Turkey	1
Bahrain	1
Hong Kong (China)	1
Singapore	1
UAE	1
Morocco	0.940
Malaysia	0.920
Kuwait	0.871
Colombia	0.851
Lebanon	0.838
China (People's Republic of)	0.824
Qatar	0.812
Albania	0.781
Thailand	0.724
Afghanistan	0.669
Azerbaijan	0.668
Cameroon	0.668
Ghana	0.667
Syrian Arab Republic	0.667
Kenya	0.667

Producers and transit points

Comparing the GTRIC-e indices with the RCAP-e and RCAT-e indices indicates that China is the main producer of counterfeit leather articles from 2017 to 2019. China exports fake leather goods all over the world (Table 4.9). Turkey was also identified as a producer of fake leather articles mainly destined for the EU.

Table 4.9. Producers of fake leather articles and handbags, 2017-19

Producing economy	Main destinations	Transport mode
China	US	Mail - Sea
	EU	Mail - Air - Sea
	Japan	Mail - Air - Sea
	Gulf countries (Saudi Arabia, Kuwait)	Sea - Rail
	Morocco	Sea - Air
	South American countries (Dominican Republic, Chile, Mexico, Puerto Rico and Uruguay)	Sea - Air
	African countries (Cabo Verde, Namibia, Senegal)	Sea
Turkey	EU	Mail - Air - Road

		US	Mail - Air
		Saudi Arabia	Mail - Air
		Dominican Republic	Air
		Australia	Air - Mail
		Kuwait	Mail - Air
		Algeria	Sea
		African countries (Angola, Congo and Gambia)	Air - Mail
Colombia		US	
		EU	Mail - Sea

Hong Kong (China), the UAE and Kuwait were identified as main transit points for the trade in fake handbags and leather articles. The UAE re-exports fake leather goods from China and Turkey worldwide. Kuwait re-exports counterfeit leather goods originating from China and Southeast Asia mainly to the EU.

Table 4.10. Key transit points for counterfeit leather articles and handbags, 2017-19

Provenance	Transit point	Destinations
China	UAE	EU
		United States
		Gulf countries (Saudi Arabia, Kuwait, UAE, Bahrain and Qatar)
		Egypt
Turkey		Jordan
		South Africa
?	Hong Kong	United States
		Japan
		Morocco
		Ukraine
		South American countries (Chile, Ecuador, Jamaica, Puerto Rico, Dominican Republic and Colombia)
		Africa (South Africa and Sierra Leone)
		Gulf countries (Saudi Arabia and Kuwait)
China	Kuwait	
		EU
India, Indonesia, Philippines, Viet Nam		
		US
Turkey		

Trade routes for fake footwear

Provenance and destination economies

According to the database on global customs seizures, China was by far the main provenance economy of counterfeit footwear between 2017 and 2019, being the origin of 79% of the total seized value of IP-infringing footwear (Figure 4.7.). It was followed by Hong Kong (China) (13%) and Turkey (3%).

Figure 4.7. Top provenance economies for counterfeit footwear, 2017-19

Share of global seized value

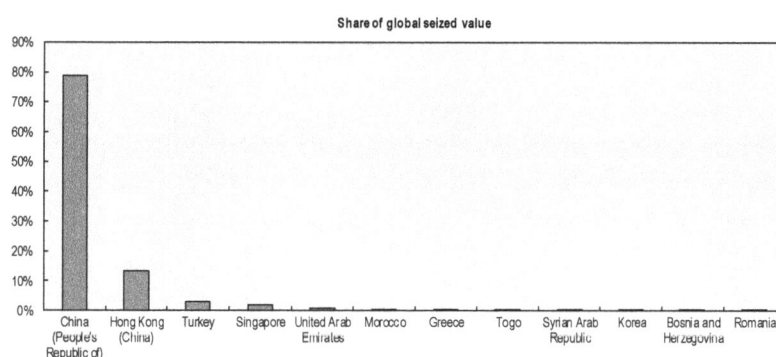

Source: OECD/EUIPO database.

The GTRIC-e indices for counterfeit footwear, which compare the customs seizures intensities for this product category with the legitimate trade intensities for each provenance economy, indicate that Hong Kong is most likely to be source of counterfeit footwear (Table 4.11). It also confirms that Singapore, the UAE, Turkey and China are part of the list of the economies most likely to export fake footwear. The GTRIC-e indices also shows that increased number of countries have participated in trade in counterfeit footwear between 2017 and 2019. This includes countries with marginal participation in trade in counterfeits in previous years such as African countries (Guinea, Nigeria, Senegal, Ghana, Cameroon), Middle East countries (Afghanistan, Bahrain, Lebanon and Iran). The seized value of counterfeit footwear originating from these economies is not significant in absolute terms, but it represents a high share of their legitimate trade flows, which make them economies with a high propensity to be a source of fake footwear. This indicates that a growing number of economies are participating to the trade in counterfeit footwear and counterfeiters are using new trade routes.

Table 4.11. Relative likelihood of an economy to be a source of fake footwear

GTRIC-e world for footwear; average 2017-19

provenance	GTRIC-e
Hong Kong (China)	1
Guinea	0.9999
Venezuela	0.9995
Singapore	0.9992
Afghanistan	0.9990
Nigeria	0.9985
UAE	0.9963
Turkey	0.9863
Bahrain	0.9761
Senegal	0.9605
Ghana	0.9573
Lebanon	0.9522
Iran	0.9038
Cameroon	0.9004
China (People's Republic of)	0.8674
Colombia	0.8051
Egypt	0.7508
Greece	0.7272

Iraq	0.6667
Mauritania	0.6667
Jordan	0.6667
Algeria	0.6659
Korea	0.5862
Georgia	0.5754

The list of top provenance economies for counterfeit footwear imported to the EU is comparable to the list for world imports of fake footwear. However, Armenia, Russia, Kazakhstan and Greece play greater roles in EU imports than in world imports.

Table 4.12. Relative likelihood of an economy to be a source of fake footwear imported to the EU, 2017-19

GTRIC-e EU for footwear to the EU; average 2017-19

Provenance	GTRIC-e
Armenia	1
Ghana	1
Guinea	1
Hong Kong (China)	1
Iran	1
Nigeria	1
Senegal	1
Togo	1
Lebanon	1
Syrian Arab Republic	1
Ecuador	0.9999
Singapore	0.9996
Turkey	0.9992
Russia	0.9954
UAE	0.9920
Kazakhstan	0.9778
Colombia	0.9768
China (People's Republic of)	0.9650
Malaysia	0.7845
Egypt	0.7165
Israel	0.7121
Greece	0.6922
Afghanistan	0.6667
Cameroon	0.6667
Algeria	0.6667

Figure 4.8., which shows the most intensive trade routes, indicates that the largest share of counterfeit footwear is exported from China to the US and the EU, as well as Algeria, Tunisia, Chile and Russia.

Figure 4.8. Top provenance-destination economies for counterfeit footwear, 2017-19

Share of global seized value

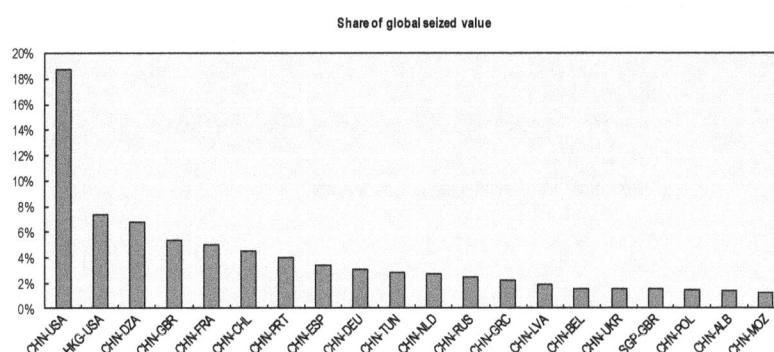

Source: OECD/EUIPO database.

Producers and transit points

Comparing the GTRIC-e indices with the RCAP-e and RCAT-e indices indicates that China were the main producer of fake footwear destined to all world regions. China exports fake footwear directly or through transit points such as the UAE. Turkey and Malaysia were also identified as producing economies. While China exports fake footwear across the world, Turkey and Malaysia targeted mostly Europe and the US.

Table 4.13. Producers of counterfeit footwear, 2017-19

Producing economy	Main destinations	Transport mode
China	EU	Mail - Air - Sea
	United States	
	Ukraine	Air - Sea
	South American countries	Sea
	Gulf countries	Sea - Rail
	Africa (North African countries, Angola, Cabo Verde, Mozambique and South Africa)	Sea - Air
	Lebanon	Sea
	Afghanistan	Mail
	Russia	Sea - Road
	Japan	Sea - Mail - Air
	Jordan	Sea
Turkey	EU	Mail - Air - Road
	Southeast of Europe (Bosnia and Herzegovina, Serbia)	Road
	United States	Mail
	Saudi Arabia	Sea - Mail
	Ukraine	Road
	North Africa	Road - Air - Sea
Malaysia	EU	Mail - Air
	Saudi Arabia	Mail - Air - Sea
	US	

Table 4.14. Key transit points for counterfeit footwear, 2017-19

Provenance	Transit point	Main destinations
Hong Kong	Hong Kong (China)	US
		EU
		South and central American countries (Colombia, Chile, Ecuador, Jamaica)
		Ukraine, Russia
		Gulf countries (Kuwait, Qatar, Saudi Arabia)
?	Singapore	EU
		US
		Russia
China	UAE	Saudi Arabia
		Kuwait , UAE, Bahrain
		South Africa, Algeria
?	Armenia	EU

Trade routes for fake toys and games

Provenance and destination economies

Data on global customs seizures indicate that China was by far the main provenance country of counterfeit toys and games, being the origin of 84.0% of the global seized value of this product category between 2017 and 2019. It was followed by Honk Kong (China) (9.0%), Argentina (2.4%) and Turkey (1.6%).

Figure 4.9. Top provenance economies for counterfeit toys and games, 2017-19

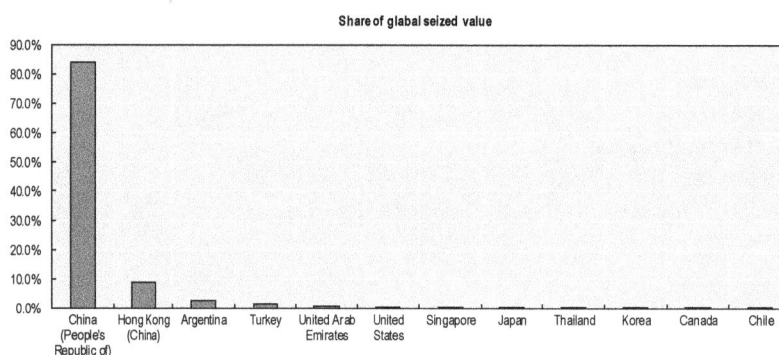

Source: OECD/EUIPO database.

The GTRIC-e indices that compare the intensities of customs seizures of counterfeit toys and games with legitimate trade intensities for each provenance economy indicate that Hong Kong is the most likely to export fake toys and games (Table 4.15). Other economies include China, Singapore, the UAE, Iran Turkey, Argentina, Ecuador and Chile.

Table 4.15. Relative likelihood of an economy to be a source of fake toys and games, 2017-19

GTRIC-e for toys and games, average 2017-19

provenance	GTRIC-e
Hong Kong (China)	1
UAE	0.978
Iran	0.951
Turkey	0.945
Singapore	0.868
China (People's Republic of)	0.693
Argentina	0.667
Ecuador	0.666
Chile	0.666
Georgia	0.526
Estonia	0.390
Korea	0.362
India	0.349
Kuwait	0.333

Table 4.16, which lists the top provenance economies of fake toys and games imported to the EU, identified from the GTRIC-e methodology, indicates that Hong Kong (China), Singapore and Turkey are the most likely to export fake toys and games to the EU. The list of the top provenance countries for the EU is comparable to the one for the world. However, it should be noted that Singapore and China play a greater role in EU imports than in world imports.

Table 4.16. Relative likelihood of an economy to be a source of fake toys and games imported into the EU, 2017-19

GTRIC-e for fake toys and games imported to the EU, average 2017-19

provenance	GTRIC-e
Hong Kong (China)	1
Singapore	1
Turkey	1
Iran	0.981
China (People's Republic of)	0.916
Ecuador	0.667
Georgia	0.538
Thailand	0.485
UAE	0.372
Azerbaijan	0.334
Iraq	0.333
Kuwait	0.333
Saudi Arabia	0.332
Suriname	0.332
Syrian Arab Republic	0.331

Regarding the most intensive trade routes, descriptive statistics of global customs seizures suggest that from 2017 to 2019, the largest share of counterfeit toys and games was exported from China to the US, the EU, Chile, Uruguay and Brazil.

Figure 4.10.Top provenance-destination economies of fake toys and games, 2017-19

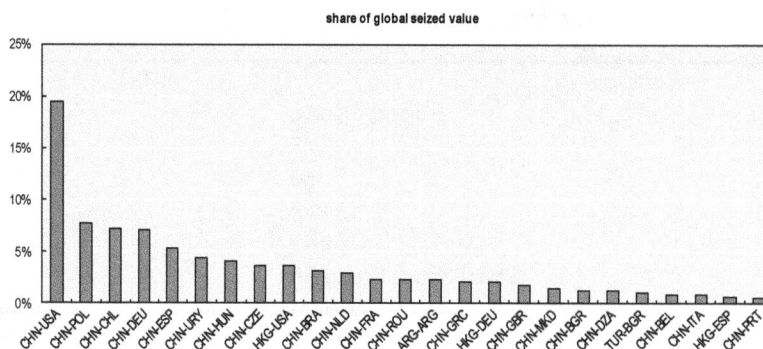

Source: OECD/EUIPO database.

Producers and transit points

Comparing the GTRIC-e indices with the RCAP-e and RCAT-e indices allows to determine China is the main producer of fake toys and games. It exports mainly to the EU, the US and Japan via mail and air, while it exports mainly by sea to the Gulf countries, Africa and South America (Table 4.17). Turkey and Korea were also identified as producing economies. While the former mainly exports fake toys and games to the EU via road and mail, the latter exports fake toys and games mainly to the US and Japan.

Table 4.17. Producers of counterfeit toys and games, 2017-19

Producing economy	Main destinations	Transport mode
China	EU	Mail - Air - Sea
	US	Mail - Air
	Chile	Sea - Air
	Japan	Mail - Air - Sea
	Gulf countries (Kuwait, Saudi Arabia)	Sea - Rail - Air
	Russia, Ukraine, Belarus	Sea - Road - Air
	North Africa (Tunisia, Morocco, Algeria)	Sea
	Dominican Republic, Uruguay	Sea
	Southeast Europe	Sea
	Africa (Senegal, Guinea-Bissau, Cabo Verde, Madagascar)	Sea
Turkey	EU	Mail - Road - Air
	US	
	Qatar	Sea
Korea	US	
	Japan	Mail
	EU	Mail - Air - Sea
	Chile	Sea

The GTRIC-e and RCAT-e indices reveal that Hong Kong (China) and Singapore are important hubs for the trade in fake toys and games. Table 4.18 shows they re-export to the EU, the US, South America, Eastern Europe and the Gulf countries.

The UAE and Saudi Arabia were also identified as transit points for the trade in fake toys and games. They appear to target the Gulf region and the EU. Moreover, fake toys and games passing through Saudi Arabia mainly come from China and the UAE.

Table 4.18. Key transit points for fake toys and games, 2017-19

Provenance	Transit point	Main destinations
?	Hong Kong (China)	US
		EU
		Japan
		Chile, Puerto Rico, Colombia
		Belarus, Ukraine
		Kuwait, Saudi Arabia
?	Singapore	EU
		US
		Brazil
		Japan
		Oman
?	UAE	Saudi Arabia, Kuwait, Qatar
		EU
		Algeria
China	Saudi Arabia	EU
UAE		Qatar, Kuwait

Trade routes for fake jewellery

Provenance and destination economies

According to the global customs seizure database, China and Hong Kong (China) were the main provenance economies of counterfeit jewellery over the 2017-19 period. Altogether, they were the origin of almost 96% of the global seized value of fake jewellery. They were followed by Thailand, Singapore and Turkey (Figure 4.11.).

Figure 4.11. Top provenance economies of counterfeit jewellery, 2017-19

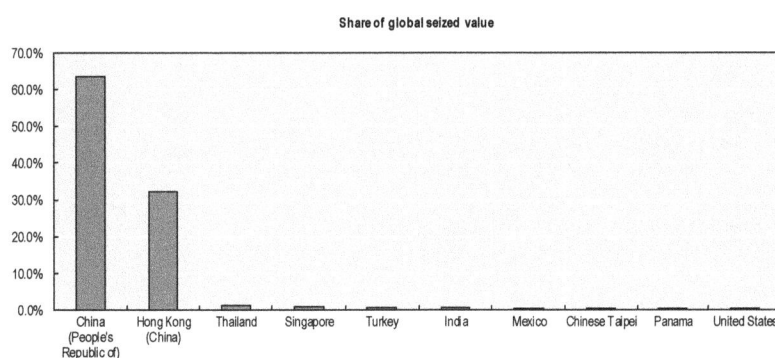

Source: OECD/EUIPO database.

The GTRIC indices which compare intensities of the trade in fake jewellery with the licit trade in jewellery confirm that China and Honk Kong (China) were the most likely to export fake jewellery over the 2017-19 period (Table 4.19).

Table 4.19. Relative likelihood of an economy to be a source of counterfeit jewellery, 2017-19

GTRIC-e for jewellery; average 2017-19

provenance	GTRIC-e
China (People's Republic of)	1
Hong Kong (China)	1
Panama	0.666
Viet Nam	0.533
Thailand	0.512
Turkey	0.491
Singapore	0.360
Bahrain	0.338
Costa Rica	0.333
Jordan	0.331
Tuvalu	0.330
Colombia	0.236
Pakistan	0.197
Mexico	0.186
Malaysia	0.171

Note: A higher score on the GTRIC index means there is a greater likelihood that the economy in question is a source of counterfeit goods.

Table 4.20. Relative likelihood of an economy to be a source of fake jewellery imported into the EU, 2017-19

GTRIC-e for jewellery to the EU; average 2017-19

provenance	GTRIC-e
Hong Kong (China)	1
China (People's Republic of)	1
Turkey	0.990
Malaysia	0.916
Benin	0.667
Qatar	0.608
Egypt	0.602
Kuwait	0.579
Thailand	0.486
Viet Nam	0.483
Ukraine	0.424
Ghana	0.405
Singapore	0.391
Cameroon	0.333

Note: A higher score on the GTRIC index means there is a greater likelihood that the economy in question is a source of counterfeit goods.

Descriptive statistics on the most intensive trade routes indicate that over the period 2017 to 2019 the largest share of counterfeit jewellery was exported from China and Hong Kong (China) to the US (Figure 4.12.). Large trade flows of counterfeit jewellery also include exports from China and Hong Kong (China) to the EU.

Figure 4.12. Top provenance-destination economies of counterfeit jewellery, 2017-19

Share of global seized value

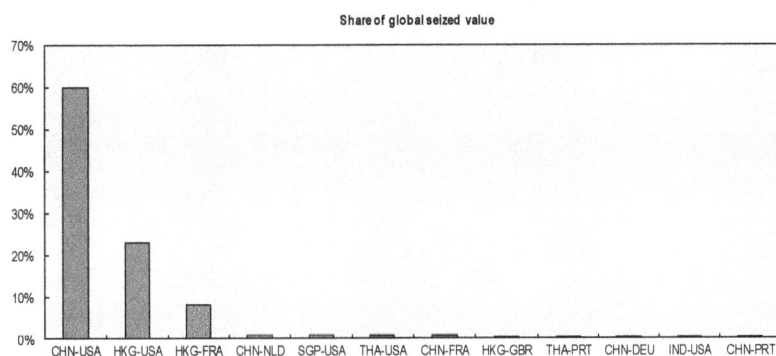

Source: OECD/EUIPO database.

Producers and transit points

The GTRIC-e indices and the RCAP-e and RCAT-e indices allowed to identify China as the main producing economy of fake jewellery. China exports fake jewellery mainly to the US, the EU, Japan, Morocco and the Gulf countries.

Thailand and Malaysia, which are important producers of counterfeit jewellery, export mainly to the EU and the US.

Table 4.21. Producers of counterfeit jewellery, 2017-19

Producing economy	Main destinations
China	US
	EU
	Morocco
	Puerto Rico
	Japan
	Saudi Arabia, Kuwait
	Ukraine
	Chile
Thailand	US
	EU
	EU
Malaysia	US

Hong Kong (China) appears as an important hub for the trade in fake jewellery, re-exporting to the US, the EU, South America, North Africa and the Gulf region. Singapore and the UAE that are two other transit points, re-exporting fake jewellery mainly to the US, the EU and the Gulf countries. Ukraine seems to be a hub for fake jewellery coming from China and destined for the EU.

Table 4.22. Key transit points of counterfeit jewellery, 2017-19

Provenance economy	Transit points	Main destinations
?	Hong Kong	US
		EU
		Puerto Rico
		Morocco
		Qatar
		Ukraine
?	Singapore	US
		EU
		Saudi Arabia
?	UAE	EU
		US
		Russia
		Saudi Arabia, Kuwait
China	Ukraine	EU

Trade routes for fake clothing

Provenance and destination economies

The database on global customs seizures indicates China was by far the main exporter of fake clothing over the period 2017 to 2019, being the origin of 62% of the total seized value of this product category (Figure 4.13.). Turkey (12%) and Hong Kong (11%) were the main provenances of fake clothing after China. Other Asian countries such as Vietnam, Bangladesh, India and Indonesia appear on the list of the top provenance economies for counterfeit clothing.

Figure 4.13. Top provenance economies for counterfeit clothing, 2017-19

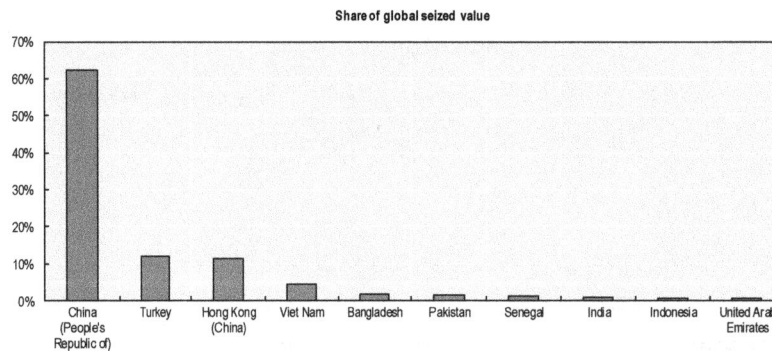

Source: OECD/EUIPO database.

The GTRIC-e indices which compare intensities of the trade in fake clothing with legitimate trade flows indicate that many countries participate in the trade of fake clothing. It confirms that Hong Kong (China), Turkey and China were the most likely to export fake clothing. The share of counterfeit goods in export of African and Middle Eastern economies was relatively high, though the total seized value of fake clothing from them is low in absolute terms but represents a high share of legitimate trade flows.

Table 4.23. Relative likelihood of an economy to be a source of fake clothing, 2017-19

GTRIC-e for clothing; average 2017-19

Provenance	GTRIC-e
Hong Kong (China)	1
Nigeria	1
Senegal	1
Iraq	1
Cameroon	1
Iran	1
Afghanistan	1
Algeria	1
Syrian Arab Republic	1
Azerbaijan	0.997
Uganda	0.992
Turkey	0.944
Venezuela	0.943
Singapore	0.868
Lebanon	0.866
UAE	0.863
Peru	0.783
China (People's Republic of)	0.771
Pakistan	0.688
Curaçao	0.667
Libya	0.667
Guinea	0.582
Ghana	0.570
Ecuador	0.488
Viet Nam	0.464

The list of economies most likely to be sources of fake clothing imported to the EU is similar to those for world imports. However, Russia, Kenya and Chile play a larger role in EU exports (Table 4.24).

Table 4.24. Relative likelihood of an economy to be source of fake clothing imported into the EU, 2017-19

GTRIC-e for clothing to the EU; average 2017-19

provenance	GTRIC-e
Azerbaijan	1
Algeria	1
Ghana	1
Iran	1
Iraq	1
Nigeria	1
Senegal	1
Syrian Arab Republic	1
Afghanistan	1
Hong Kong (China)	1
Singapore	0.998
Kenya	0.991
Lebanon	0.990
Russia	0.981

UAE	0.957
Turkey	0.957
Chile	0.810
Colombia	0.788
China (People's Republic of)	0.778
United States	0.745
Cameroon	0.667
Libya	0.667
Togo	0.667
Guinea	0.667
Paraguay	0.645

Figure 4.14., which represents the most intensive routes of fake clothing, shows diversified flows with many economies implicated. It reveals that the largest share of fake clothing came from China and was destined for Brazil. It also included flows from China to the EU and the US, Hong Kong to the US and the EU, Turkey to the EU and Vietnam to the EU and the US.

Figure 4.14. Top provenance-destination economies for counterfeit clothing, 2017-19

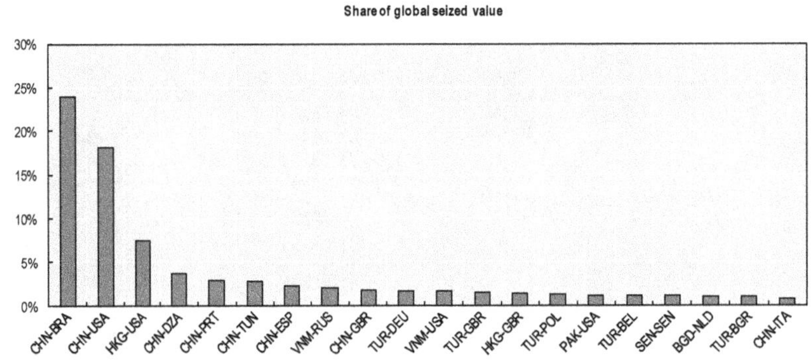

Share of global seized value

Source: OECD/EUIPO database.

Producers and transit points

Analysing the GTRIC-e indices as well as the RCAP-e and RCAT-e indices allows to identify China as the main producer of counterfeit clothing from 2017 to 2019 (see Table 4.25). China exports fake clothing directly worldwide or through transit points like Ukraine and the UAE.

Turkey was also identified as a producing economy, directly exporting counterfeit clothing mainly to the EU and Southeast Europe or through transit points such as Ukraine. Thailand and India also appear to be important producers of fake clothing and export to the EU and the US.

Table 4.25. Producers of counterfeit clothing, 2017-19

Producing economy	Main destinations
China	US
	EU
	Ukraine (transit point)
	Japan
	South America (Dominican Republic, Mexico, Chile, Brazil, Puerto Rico)
	Russia
	Gulf countries (Saudi Arabia, Kuwait, UAE – transit point)
	Southeast Europe (Bosnia and Herzegovina, Albania, Serbia, Kosovo)
	African countries (North Africa, South Africa, Cabo Verde, Mozambique, Tanzania, Uganda, Senegal)
Turkey	EU
	US
	Ukraine (transit point)
	Southeast Europe
	Russia
	Kuwait
	Australia
	Algeria
Thailand	US
	EU
	Mali
	Japan
India	EU
	US
	Libya
	Saudi Arabia

Honk Kong (China) appears to be an important transit point for trade in counterfeit clothing, re-exporting it worldwide. Singapore and the UAE, which are also listed as hubs, re-export fake clothing to the EU, the US and Gulf countries. Finally, Ukraine seems to receive fake clothing from China and Turkey and re-exports it to EU and the US exclusively.

Table 4.26. Transit points for counterfeit clothing, 2017-19

Provenance	Transit point	Main destinations
China	Hong Kong (China)	US
		EU
		Suriname, Colombia, Jamaica, Chile, Ecuador
		Colombia
		Japan
		Ukraine
		Algeria
		Qatar
		Sierra Leone
?	Singapore	US
		EU
		Saudi Arabia
China	UAE	EU
		Saudi Arabia
		US
China	Ukraine	EU
Turkey		US

Estimating the total value of the trade in counterfeit and pirated goods

While the GTRIC does not give a direct measure of the overall magnitude of counterfeiting and piracy in world trade, it establishes relationships that can be useful. Specifically, the GTRIC matrix can be used to approximate the international trade in counterfeit and pirated goods.

For each good coming from a given provenance economy, the GTRIC assigns a probability of it being counterfeit relative to the most intensive combination of the product and the provenance economy. In theory, the absolute number of counterfeit trades for one product from a provenance economy can be integrated into the corresponding cell of the GTRIC matrix to yield the total value of world trade in the counterfeit and pirated product (see Annex B for more details).

However, determining this total value is currently impossible for two main reasons. First, the clandestine and changing nature of the trade in counterfeits makes any measurement exercise extremely difficult and highly imprecise, and second, operational data from customs offices are in most cases strictly confidential.

Nevertheless, the GTRIC matrix can be employed to gauge the ceiling value for the international trade in counterfeit and pirated goods. As in the (OECD/EUIPO, 2016[1]) report, this approach is taken by establishing an upper limit for the trade in counterfeits (in percentages) from the key provenance economies in product categories that are most vulnerable to counterfeiting. These values are called fixed points.

The last step in the analysis is to move from the relative intensities of counterfeiting to gauging the absolute values of counterfeit and pirated products in international trade. To do this, at least one probability of containing counterfeit and pirated products in a given product category from at least one provenance economy must be identified. Importantly, this identification must be based on information other than customs seizure data, given the several methodological biases these data suffer from.

In the 2008 study, this fixed point was determined based on ex ante assumptions that were debated with industry and enforcement representatives. At the time, this was the best possible methodological approach given the poor data quality.

For the analysis presented in the (OECD/EUIPO, 2016[1]) study, a set of confidential and structured interviews with customs officials was carried out. These interviews resulted in a large number of detailed quantitative and qualitative sets of information on customs operations that in turn allowed this report to determine the upper limit of the absolute number of imported counterfeit and pirated goods. Eventually, the fixed point was set at 27% for HS64 (footwear) from China.

For the present study, the fixed point used in the (OECD/EUIPO, 2016[1]) study was re-examined based on a focus group meeting and on interviews with customs officials from several EU member countries. These interviews confirmed that the fixed point picked for the analysis presented in the (OECD/EUIPO, 2016[1]) study is still relevant. Consequently, this fixed point was also used in the present analysis.

Of course, such a fixed point does not imply that on average 27% of footwear exported from China is counterfeit: it represents the upper level of a potential trade in counterfeits, meaning that within the HS64 category imported from China by some EU members, the share of counterfeits reached 27% in certain years. This result could then be extrapolated onto the yearly trade flows, which would give a basis to be applied to the GTRIC. Consequently, the results presented in this study refer to the upper possible limit of the trade in counterfeit and pirated goods.

The best estimates of this study, based on customs seizure data, indicate that counterfeit and pirated goods amounted to as much as USD 464 billion in world trade in 2019. It is important to note that this amount refers to the upper limit of the trade counterfeits. Consequently, as much as 2.5% of total world trade in 2019 was in counterfeit and pirated goods (Figure 4.15.).

Figure 4.15. Estimates of global trade in counterfeit and pirated goods, 2017-19

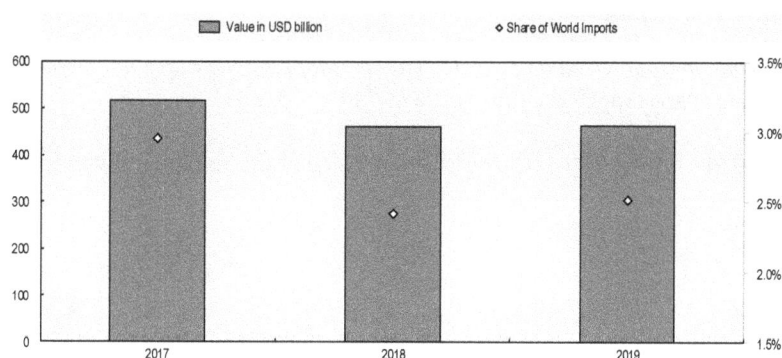

Source: OECD/EUIPO database

References

OCDE (2008), *The Economic Impact of Counterfeiting and Piracy*, Éditions OCDE, Paris, https://doi.org/10.1787/9789264045521-en. [9]

OCDE/EUIPO (2021), *Misuse of Containerized Maritime Shipping in the Global Trade of Counterfeits*, Éditions OCDE, Paris,, https://doi.org/10.1787/e39d8939-en. [8]

OECD (2021), *COVID-19 vaccine and the Threat of Illicit Trade, Chair's Summary Note*, https://www.oecd.org/gov/illicit-trade/summary-note-covid-19-vaccine-and-the-threat-of-illicit-trade.pdf. [12]

OECD (2020), *Illicit Trade in a Time of Crisis. Chair's Summary Note*, https://www.oecd.org/gov/illicit-trade/oecd-webinar-illicit-trade-time-crisis-23-april.pdf. [10]

OECD (2020), *Trade in Fake Medicines at the Time of the Covid-19 Pandemics. Chair's Summary Note*, https://www.oecd.org/gov/illicit-trade/oecd-fake-medicines-webinar-june-10-summary-note.pdf. [14]

OECD (2018), *Governance Frameworks to Counter Illicit Trade*, OECD Publishing, Paris,, https://doi.org/10.1787/9789264291652-en. [13]

OECD/EUIPO (2020), *Trade in Counterfeit Pharmaceutical Products*, Illicit Trade, OECD Publishing, Paris, https://dx.doi.org/10.1787/a7c7e054-en. [7]

OECD/EUIPO (2019), *Trends in Trade in Counterfeit and Pirated Goods*, OECD Publishing, Paris,, https://doi.org/10.1787/g2g9f533-en. [3]

OECD/EUIPO (2018), *Misuse of Small Parcels for Trade in Counterfeit Goods: Facts and Trends*, OECD Publishing, Paris, https://doi.org/10.1787/9789264307858-en. [6]

OECD/EUIPO (2018), *Trade in Counterfeit Goods and Free Trade Zones: Evidence from Recent Trends*, OECD Publishing, Paris/EUIPO, Alicante, https://doi.org/10.1787/9789264289550-en. [4]

OECD/EUIPO (2018), *Why Do Countries Export Fakes?: The Role of Governance Frameworks, Enforcement and Socio-economic Factors*, OECD Publishing, Paris/EUIPO, Alicante, https://doi.org/10.1787/9789264302464-en. [5]

OECD/EUIPO (2017), *Mapping the Real Routes of Trade in Fake Goods, Illicit Trade*, OECD Publishing, Paris, https://doi.org/10.1787/9789264278349-en. [2]

OECD/EUIPO (2016), *Trade in Counterfeit and Pirated Goods: Mapping the Economic Impact, Illicit Trade*, OECD Publishing, Paris, https://doi.org/10.1787/9789264252653-en. [1]

UNICRI (2020), *"Cyber-crime during the COVID-19 Pandemic"*, http://www.unicri.it/news/cyber-crime-during-covid-19-pandemic. [11]

Chapter 5. The European Union case study

IP intensity of the EU economy

Intellectual property rights are of fundamental importance for the competitiveness of the EU economy as a whole. At the macroeconomic level, the IP-intensive industries have generated on average 45% of the EU GDP between 2014 and 2016. This corresponds to EUR 6.6 trillion annually. In addition, IP-intensive industries contributed directly to 29.2% of employment.

Table 5.1. Contribution of IP-intensive industries to GDP in the EU, 2014-16 average

IPR intensive industries	Value added/GDP (EUR million)	Share of total EU GDP (%)
Trade mark-intensive	5,447,857	37.3%
Design-intensive	2,371,282	16.2%
Patent-intensive	2,353,560	16.1%
Copyright-intensive	1,008,383	6.9%
Geographical indication-intensive	20,155	0.1%
Plant variety -intensive	181,570	1.2%
All IPR-intensive	**6,551,768**	**44.8%**

Source: EPO-EUIPO (2019), "IPR-intensive industries and economic performance in the European Union", Industry-Level Analysis Report, September 2019, Third edition.

Table 5.2. Direct and indirect contribution of IPR-intensive industries to employment, 2014-16 average

IPR intensive industries	Employment (direct)	Share of total employment (direct) (%)	Employment (direct + indirect)	Share of total employment (direct + indirect) (%)
Trade mark-intensive	46,700,950	21.7%	65,047,936	30.2%
Design-intensive	30,711,322	14.2%	45,073,288	20.9%
Patent-intensive	23,571,234	10.9%	34,740,674	16.1%
Copyright-intensive	11,821,456	5.5%	15,358,044	7.1%
GI-intensive	n/a	n/a	399,324	0.2%
PVR-intensive	1,736,407	0.8%	2,618,502	1.2%
All IPR-intensive	**62,962,766**	**29.2%**	**83,807,505**	**38.9%**

Source: EPO-EUIPO (2019), "IPR-intensive industries and economic performance in the European Union", Industry-Level Analysis Report, September 2019, Third edition.

A recent report by the EUIPO and the EPO, covering the period 2007-2019, delves deeper into the role of IPRs for individual firms. It analyses a representative sample of over 127 000 European firms from all 27 EU member states and the UK. According to this report, firms that own IPRs generate 20% higher revenues per employee in comparison to their counterparts without an IPR portfolio. Firms that own IPRs also pay on average 19% higher wages than firms that do not. The premium associated with IPR ownership is particularly high for SMEs and firms registering bundles of IPRs.

IPRs provide incentives for investment in R&D, innovation, and development of intangible assets. Therefore, IP protection is of crucial importance for stimulating growth and economic development in advanced economies such as the economies of EU Member States.

Imports of fakes to the EU: the updated picture

As shown in Table 5.3, imports of fake goods to the EU were most likely luxury goods, with articles of leather and handbags, footwear, watches, clothing and jewellery having the highest propensity to be counterfeited. Intermediary products imported to the EU such as toys and games, electronic goods and auto spare parts were also subject to counterfeiting.

Apart from luxury goods, EU customs officers reported significant volumes of fake goods that pose health and safety issues entering the EU. Products like toys and games, perfumery and cosmetics or spare auto parts – which are all manufactured by industries ranked among the top 15 most sensitive – can be dangerous for consumers, as often they do not meet sanitary or security standards.

Table 5.3. Top 15 EU industries likely to be targeted for counterfeit imports, 2017-19

GTRIC-p for the EU, average 2017-19

HS Code	GTRIC-p
Articles of leather; handbags (42)	1
Footwear (64)	1
Watches (91)	1
Clothing, knitted or crocheted (61)	1
Toys and games (95)	1
Knitted or crocheted fabrics (60)	0.999
Jewellery (71)	0.999
Perfumery and cosmetics (33)	0.997
Tobacco (24)	0.952
Optical; photographic; medical apparatus (90)	0.893
Electrical machinery and electronics (85)	0.676
Musical instruments (92)	0.669
Clothing and accessories, not knitted or crocheted (62/65)	0.583
Miscellaneous manufactured articles (66/67/96)	0.549
Vehicles (87)	0.205

Source: OECD calculations.

The list of the top 15 EU industries most likely to be targeted for counterfeit imports from 2017 to 2019 is comparable to the one from 2014 to 2016. However, the descriptions of customs seizures indicate that counterfeiters are continually adapting their strategies. The main change over this period has been the increase in the propensity of the jewellery sector (HS 71) to be targeted and the decrease in prevalence of other manufactured articles (HS 66/67/96).

Figure 5.1. Changes in propensities for products categories in EU imports to be targeted for counterfeiting

GTRIC-p for the EU, averages 2014-16 and 2017-19

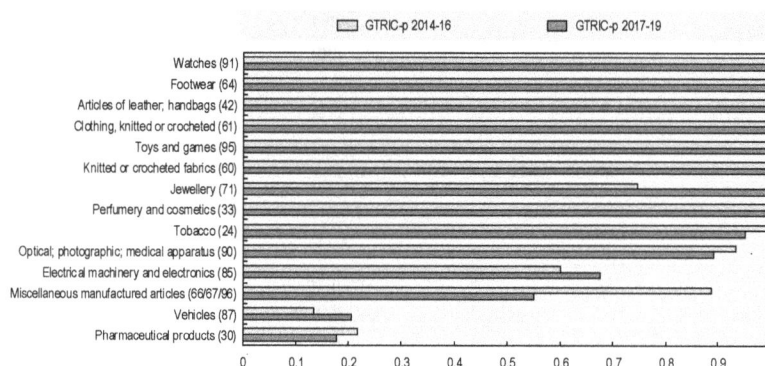

Source: OECD/EUIPO database.

Figure 5.2 compares the industrial composition of the trade in counterfeits globally with EU imports for 2017 to 2019. Despite the fact there is a wide range of counterfeit goods destined for both global and EU markets, some differences can be highlighted. Tobacco, clothing and accessories not knitted or crocheted were less targeted in EU trade than in world trade. Conversely, counterfeit optical, photographic and medical apparatuses (HS 90) – the interceptions in this category are mainly sunglasses – and knitted or crocheted fabrics are more prevalent in EU trade than in world trade. Industries such as beverages (HS 22) and pharmaceuticals (HS 30) are also more prevalent in EU trade than in world trade, placing citizens at substantial risk.

Figure 5.2. Comparing the industrial composition of the trade in counterfeits globally with EU imports, 2017-19

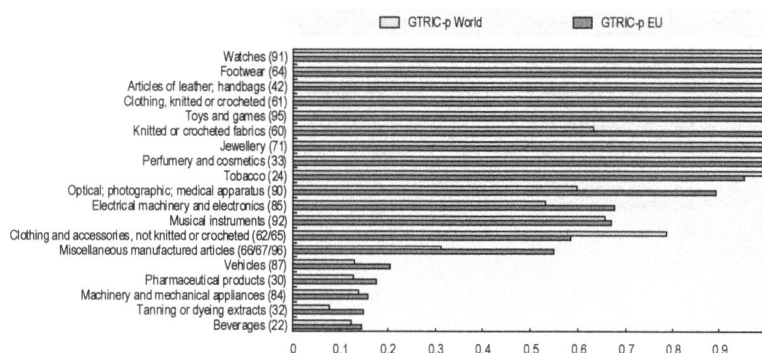

Source: OECD/EUIPO database.

Regarding the provenance economies of counterfeit goods destined to the EU, the GTRIC-e index shows that the scope is large, with provenances located in all world regions. The propensity to export counterfeits to the EU was the highest for Benin, Hong Kong (China), the Syrian Arab Republic and Afghanistan. They were closely followed by Senegal, China, Turkey and the UAE.

Table 5.4 Top 20 provenance economies of counterfeit goods entering the EU, 2017-19

GTRIC-e for the EU, average 2017-19

Provenance economy	GTRIC-e
Benin	1
Hong Kong (China)	1
Syrian Arab Republic	1
Afghanistan	1
Senegal	0.9997
China (People's Republic of)	0.9986
Turkey	0.0063
UAE	0.9956
Georgia	0.9745
Lebanon	0.9355
Iran	0.9019
Morocco	0.8573
Bangladesh	0.8316
Singapore	0.8284
Togo	0.6835
Albania	0.6767
Cameroon	0.6353
Madagascar	0.6106
Thailand	0.6090

Figure 5.3. Changes in exports to the EU from provenance economies

GTRIC-p for the EU, averages 2014-16 and 2017-19

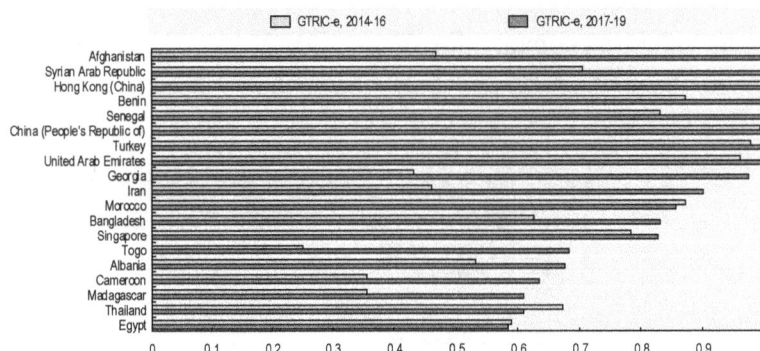

Source: OECD/EUIPO database.

Estimates of counterfeit and pirated imports to the EU

Estimates based on the GTRIC methodology indicate that total trade in counterfeit and pirated goods destined to the EU amounted to as much as USD 134 billion (EUR 119 billion) in 2019. This number implies that as much as 5.8% of EU imports were in counterfeit and pirated products.

References

OCDE (2008), *The Economic Impact of Counterfeiting and Piracy*, Éditions OCDE, Paris, https://doi.org/10.1787/9789264045521-en. [9]

OCDE/EUIPO (2021), *Misuse of Containerized Maritime Shipping in the Global Trade of Counterfeits*, Éditions OCDE, Paris,, https://doi.org/10.1787/e39d8939-en. [8]

OECD (2021), *COVID-19 vaccine and the Threat of Illicit Trade, Chair's Summary Note*, https://www.oecd.org/gov/illicit-trade/summary-note-covid-19-vaccine-and-the-threat-of-illicit-trade.pdf. [12]

OECD (2020), *Illicit Trade in a Time of Crisis. Chair's Summary Note*, https://www.oecd.org/gov/illicit-trade/oecd-webinar-illicit-trade-time-crisis-23-april.pdf. [10]

OECD (2020), *Trade in Fake Medicines at the Time of the Covid-19 Pandemics. Chair's Summary Note*, https://www.oecd.org/gov/illicit-trade/oecd-fake-medicines-webinar-june-10-summary-note.pdf. [14]

OECD (2018), *Governance Frameworks to Counter Illicit Trade*, OECD Publishing, Paris,, https://doi.org/10.1787/9789264291652-en. [13]

OECD/EUIPO (2020), *Trade in Counterfeit Pharmaceutical Products*, Illicit Trade, OECD Publishing, Paris, https://dx.doi.org/10.1787/a7c7e054-en. [7]

OECD/EUIPO (2019), *Trends in Trade in Counterfeit and Pirated Goods*, OECD Publishing, Paris,, https://doi.org/10.1787/g2g9f533-en. [3]

OECD/EUIPO (2018), *Misuse of Small Parcels for Trade in Counterfeit Goods: Facts and Trends*, OECD Publishing, Paris, https://doi.org/10.1787/9789264307858-en. [6]

OECD/EUIPO (2018), *Trade in Counterfeit Goods and Free Trade Zones: Evidence from Recent Trends*, OECD Publishing, Paris/EUIPO, Alicante, https://doi.org/10.1787/9789264289550-en. [4]

OECD/EUIPO (2018), *Why Do Countries Export Fakes?: The Role of Governance Frameworks, Enforcement and Socio-economic Factors*, OECD Publishing, Paris/EUIPO, Alicante, https://doi.org/10.1787/9789264302464-en. [5]

OECD/EUIPO (2017), *Mapping the Real Routes of Trade in Fake Goods, Illicit Trade*, OECD Publishing, Paris, https://doi.org/10.1787/9789264278349-en. [2]

OECD/EUIPO (2016), *Trade in Counterfeit and Pirated Goods: Mapping the Economic Impact, Illicit Trade*, OECD Publishing, Paris, https://doi.org/10.1787/9789264252653-en. [1]

UNICRI (2020), *"Cyber-crime during the COVID-19 Pandemic"*, http://www.unicri.it/news/cyber-crime-during-covid-19-pandemic. [11]

Chapter 6. The trade in counterfeits during the pandemic

The ongoing COVID-19 pandemic has triggered an enormous crisis that has had and will continue to have a significant impact on the illicit trade in counterfeit goods. Closures of some businesses and disruptions in transport methods have led to significant distortions in supply chains. In all these cases, criminals have leveraged these opportunities to make illicit profits.

The situation is dynamic, and it is too early to conclude the overall effect the pandemic has had on the illicit trade in fake goods. However, exchanges with enforcement officials and industry representatives, plus ongoing reports, have allowed to tease out certain trends:

- an intensified misuse of the online environment because of lockdowns and broken supply chains
- a change in the structure of trade in fakes
- a change in enforcement priorities.

Channels of transmission

As for the short-term effects, several COVID-related factors have shaped the landscape of the illicit trade in fakes. These include heavy restrictions imposed on global transport and a disruption in distribution chains due to lockdowns and health concerns.

At the same time, COVID-19 has also resulted in changes in customs control priorities (e.g. a focus on COVID-19-related products) and labour shortages among law enforcement officials. Unfortunately, these factors have reduced enforcement efforts to counter the illicit trade in many counterfeit products.

Customs and police have continued to enforce borders during the crisis. However, rapidly changing illicit networks have made informative risk profiling very difficult for customs. This shows further efforts are required to raise awareness among enforcement officials.

Effects

Several areas where the COVID-19 pandemic has already had a short-term effect on the trade in counterfeit goods have been scoped. These include the emergence of new routes for illicit trade, a boom in the misuse of the online environment and growth in counterfeiting in several sectors.

In the medium and longer terms, the COVID-19 pandemic will likely have a number of other effects on illicit trade. The economic downturn and continued disruptions in supply chains will undoubtedly create additional opportunities for criminals and will most likely lead to a substantial change in illicit trade volumes, routes and the composition of goods in the medium term. A rise in cybercrime will keep shifting attention to the online environment. In addition, limits on air transport and more compliance that is expected in global value chains will re-shape the trade routes and patterns for illicit trade, which might also lead to increased misuse of FTZs. Moreover, this may lead to the emergence of more secured and compliant major trade lanes and so-called trade super highways.

New trade routes

Criminal networks have reacted quickly to the crisis and have adapted their strategies to take advantage of the shifting landscape. Counterfeiters have continued to supply counterfeits during the lockdowns in the EU and the US. It shows that these well-organized criminal networks foresaw the disruptions of some transport routes and have managed their operations accordingly. Of course, these criminal groups also benefited because different world regions were not all affected by the pandemic simultaneously. Consequently, they could draw lessons from those regions hit first (e.g. East Asia).

Abuse of the online environment

Another observed trend is a substantial shift towards further misuse of the online environment. There is robust growth in the supply of fakes on all types of online platforms, including those that used to be relatively free from this risk (OECD, 2021[12]).

Due to lockdowns in many countries, people have been using the Internet more than ever before, with the overall rate of digitization skyrocketing. The intensity of the misuse of the online environment keeps growing, and fakes tend to be increasingly found new online sites and platforms, including social media. For example, between 2020 and 2021 e-commerce activity in the US has grown by almost 40%. This has resulted in a massive growth in the supply of all sorts of counterfeits online ((OECD, 2020[10]), (UNICRI, 2020[11]).

Lockdowns have led to e-commerce becoming one of the main means of procuring fake and substandard medicines. Enforcement officials also highlight that counterfeit medical products related to COVID-19 are often bought online and shipped by air cargo in small parcels. Most of these products are produced in China and India, while Hong Kong and Singapore remain the main transit hubs ((OECD/EUIPO, 2020[7]), (OECD, 2021[12]).

Key sectors targeted

Criminals are clearly taking advantage of the global pandemic. Pharmaceuticals, medical supplies, fast-moving consumer goods (FMCG) and sectors such as tobacco or alcohol, which criminals frequently singled out before the pandemic, are all potential targets of counterfeiters.

Pharmaceuticals

The pandemic triggered a dramatic growth in the demand for pharmaceuticals and personal protective equipment (PPE) such as gloves or sanitizers. This demand was sometimes not met due to closures of borders, distortions in supply chains or insufficient production capacities. Criminals entered this niche, not only offering fake PPE but also counterfeit equipment to produce PPE or spare machine parts. Counterfeiters tend to brand fake PPE, even when the rights holder does not supply the PPE in question. Such fakes can lead to significant health and safety risks ((OECD/EUIPO, 2020[7]).

According to industry experts, the illicit trade in fake medicines keeps growing. Interviews with industry experts point to an overall growth of 5% in the average seizure value in 2020 compared with 2019. Considering the overall drop in enforcement, this suggests that the trade in illicit medicines has grown by 25% from 2019. Of these 45% are counterfeits and 55% are stolen. These findings are confirmed by the results of enforcement operations. For example, the Europol-coordinated operation SHIELD resulted in massive seizures of counterfeit medicines and doping substances.[1]

The introduction of substandard or counterfeit products into the legitimate supply chain poses grave threats to public health and safety and the efforts to combat the spread of COVID-19. This collateral damage might grow in the future, as the pandemic's economic fallout is likely to reduce patients' purchasing power worldwide.

Food, tobacco and alcohol

Additional volumes of illegal food, tobacco and alcohol have been entering markets during the COVID-19 pandemic through vulnerable supply chains and porous borders. Closures of some businesses and disruptions in transport methods have led to significant distortions in supply chains. These distortions have been generating both excess supplies of goods (e.g. closures in the food industry) and unsatisfied demand (e.g. limited access to existing suppliers). In all these cases, criminals have exploited these opportunities for illicit profits.

Regarding the illicit trade in food, enforcement officials have provided illustrative examples of new, sometimes unexpected mechanisms that have generated an additional influx of illicit food in markets. Recent targeted actions in Europe have revealed many cases of criminals infiltrating legal supply chains with substandard or counterfeit food products. Enforcement officers from the European Union Agency for Law Enforcement Cooperation (Europol) working as part of operation OPSON ("food" in ancient Greek) confiscated 12 thousand tonnes of substandard food and stopped operations of nine organized criminal groups in 2020.

For example, criminals froze large volumes of excess milk and dairy products, which resulted from lower demand, and then sold them on the market. Another example is counterfeiters adding chlorophyll and beta-carotene to substandard seed oil and then selling it as extra virgin olive oil. Horsemeat from illegal horse slaughtering, involving forging of transportation documents for animals, was also confiscated. In all these cases the illicit food was substandard and could have posed significant health risks to consumers.

Officials have highlighted a recent sharp increase in seizures of fake cigarettes, including seizures of containers filled with illicit cigarettes. There were also seizures of tobacco production equipment in several EU countries. For example in Spain, the Guardia Civil has dismantled large, clandestine factory producing and supplying counterfeit tobacco products.[2] These instances point to preparations made by criminal gangs to increase the supply of illicit tobacco. ,

Lastly, the evidence also points to strong growth in the trade and production of illicit alcohol, wine. Demand for alcohol has remained relatively stable throughout the pandemic. Nonetheless, the supply of licit alcohol is limited: supply chains are often broken, a lot of retail shops were closed during lockdowns, and policymakers often limit alcohol consumption. This gap between demand and supply is exploited by criminals who continue to supply counterfeit alcohol that is often substandard (TRACIT, 2021). For example, in Europe the production of substandard wine has been booming. Enforcement officials reported the forging of labels or production of inferior quality wine.

References

OCDE (2008), *The Economic Impact of Counterfeiting and Piracy*, Éditions OCDE, Paris, https://doi.org/10.1787/9789264045521-en. [9]

OCDE/EUIPO (2021), *Misuse of Containerized Maritime Shipping in the Global Trade of Counterfeits*, Éditions OCDE, Paris,, https://doi.org/10.1787/e39d8939-en. [8]

OECD (2021), *COVID-19 vaccine and the Threat of Illicit Trade, Chair's Summary Note*, https://www.oecd.org/gov/illicit-trade/summary-note-covid-19-vaccine-and-the-threat-of-illicit-trade.pdf. [12]

OECD (2020), *Illicit Trade in a Time of Crisis. Chair's Summary Note*, https://www.oecd.org/gov/illicit-trade/oecd-webinar-illicit-trade-time-crisis-23-april.pdf. [10]

OECD (2020), *Trade in Fake Medicines at the Time of the Covid-19 Pandemics. Chair's Summary Note*, https://www.oecd.org/gov/illicit-trade/oecd-fake-medicines-webinar-june-10-summary-note.pdf. [14]

OECD (2018), *Governance Frameworks to Counter Illicit Trade*, OECD Publishing, Paris,, https://doi.org/10.1787/9789264291652-en. [13]

OECD/EUIPO (2020), *Trade in Counterfeit Pharmaceutical Products*, Illicit Trade, OECD Publishing, Paris, https://dx.doi.org/10.1787/a7c7e054-en. [7]

OECD/EUIPO (2019), *Trends in Trade in Counterfeit and Pirated Goods*, OECD Publishing, Paris,, https://doi.org/10.1787/g2g9f533-en. [3]

OECD/EUIPO (2018), *Misuse of Small Parcels for Trade in Counterfeit Goods: Facts and Trends*, OECD Publishing, Paris, https://doi.org/10.1787/9789264307858-en. [6]

OECD/EUIPO (2018), *Trade in Counterfeit Goods and Free Trade Zones: Evidence from Recent Trends*, OECD Publishing, Paris/EUIPO, Alicante, https://doi.org/10.1787/9789264289550-en. [4]

OECD/EUIPO (2018), *Why Do Countries Export Fakes?: The Role of Governance Frameworks, Enforcement and Socio-economic Factors*, OECD Publishing, Paris/EUIPO, Alicante, https://doi.org/10.1787/9789264302464-en. [5]

OECD/EUIPO (2017), *Mapping the Real Routes of Trade in Fake Goods, Illicit Trade*, OECD Publishing, Paris, https://doi.org/10.1787/9789264278349-en. [2]

OECD/EUIPO (2016), *Trade in Counterfeit and Pirated Goods: Mapping the Economic Impact, Illicit Trade*, OECD Publishing, Paris, https://doi.org/10.1787/9789264252653-en. [1]

UNICRI (2020), *"Cyber-crime during the COVID-19 Pandemic"*, http://www.unicri.it/news/cyber-crime-during-covid-19-pandemic. [11]

Notes

1 See https://www.europol.europa.eu/newsroom/news/medicines-and-doping-substances-worth-%E2%82%AC73-million-seized-in-europe-wide-operation

2 See https://www.lavanguardia.com/sucesos/20200220/473667314907/fabrica-clandestina-underground-europa.html

Chapter 7. Concluding remarks

This study presents the updated quantitative analysis of the value, scope and magnitude of world trade in counterfeit and pirated products, using the same GTRIC methodology as in the previous (OECD/EUIPO, 2016[1]) and (OECD/EUIPO, 2019[3]) reports. In 2019 international trade in counterfeit and pirated products amounted to as much as USD 464 billion. This figure excludes domestically produced and consumed counterfeit and pirated products, and pirated digital products distributed via the Internet. It represents up to 2.5% of world trade, compared with estimates of up to 3.3% of world trade in 2016 and 2.5% in 2013.

Given these sustained levels of counterfeit goods traded globally, the intensity of counterfeiting and piracy continuous to be a great risk, with significant potential for IP theft in a knowledge-based, open and globalised economy.

The quantitative analysis in this report confirms that fake products can be found in a large and growing number of industries. This includes common consumer goods (e.g. footwear, handbags, cosmetics and toys), business-to-business products (e.g. car spare parts and chemicals), IT goods (e.g. phones, chargers and batteries) and luxury items (e.g. fashion apparel or deluxe watches).

Importantly, many of these goods can pose big health, safety and environmental risks. Fake products such as dental equipment, pharmaceuticals or baby formulas are continuously being supplied to markets through multiple channels. Moreover, the degree of consumer deception is still the highest for these classes of products.

In terms of provenance, counterfeit and pirated goods originate from virtually all economies on all continents. While the scope of provenance economies is broad, seizure statistics show that most interceptions originate from a relatively concentrated set of provenance economies. In other words, some economies tend to dominate the global trade in counterfeit and pirated goods. The highest number of counterfeit shipments being seized originates from East Asia, with China and Hong Kong (China) ranking at the top.

We have also examined the complex routes through which counterfeit and pirated goods are traded, focusing on six main product types, which are particularly vulnerable to counterfeiting. These include such consumer goods as perfumery and cosmetics, footwear, clothing, jewellery and toys. Significantly, counterfeit goods in these sectors can often pose serious health and safety risks to unaware users.

The data reveals some general patterns. Overall, China emerges as the key producer of counterfeit goods in all product categories. Several East Asian economies – including India, Thailand and Malaysia – have been identified as important producers in some sectors, although their role is much less significant than China. Finally, Turkey appears to be a relatively important producer, especially for fake leather goods and cosmetics shipped to the EU.

The estimates indicate that the total trade in fakes destined to the EU amounted to as much as USD 134 billion (EUR 119 billion) in 2019. This number implies that as much as 5.8% of EU imports were counterfeit and pirated products. From the EU perspective, China is the major producer of counterfeit and pirated products across all categories analysed for the EU Common Market.

The COVID-19 pandemic has affected the trade in fake goods, and in most cases the crisis has aggravated the existing trends. A key development is the intense misuse of the online environment, as consumers in countries locked down have turned to online markets to fulfil their needs. This has resulted in massive growth of the online supply of all sorts of counterfeits. This sharp increase in fakes concerns not only medicines and PPE but many other goods, including watches, consumer goods and electrical machinery and electronics (e.g. kitchen appliances).

The quantitative analysis presented in this report is based primarily on a quantitative assessment using the tailored statistical methodologies developed and drawing on data from a large dataset from customs seizures of IP-infringing goods. The data refer to the pre-COVID-19 period, as the crisis has significantly changed the international context, and no final conclusions can be drawn at this stage.

Directions for future work

More in-depth analyses will be crucial for developing efficient enforcement and governance frameworks to counter the substantial risks posed. This includes (i) examining the health and safety threats posed by counterfeits and (ii) the economic features of destination economies, including the quantitative relationship between the intensities of counterfeiting and free trade indices, the quality of governance and public sector integrity.

Regarding the first point, the current study shows that a large volume of counterfeits can pose serious health and safety or environmental risks. More evidence is needed on the value of the trade in such counterfeit goods. Experts must also analyse the changes in the volumes and the composition of these products, and map key trade routes. Such information could be leveraged by policymakers in awareness campaigns and would highlight the need take anti-counterfeiting into account when shaping health and environmental policies, for example.

Secondly, more quantitative research is needed to improve the understanding of factors that shape the role of destination economies in the trade in counterfeit and pirated goods. More analysis is required to develop a fuller quantitative picture of the trade in counterfeits at the national level and shed some light on factors that determine the profiles of destination economies. The analysis could, for example, investigate the quantitative relationship between the volumes of fakes entering a given economy and its socio-economic profile, as well as the quality of governance and the integrity of the public sector.

In addition to these two areas discussed above, the analysis presented could be used to help develop a more effective set of enforcement and governance responses for both transit points and producing economies. Among the issues to be addressed are the adequacy of penalties, trade-based money laundering and other factors related to transnational crime. This work could additionally leverage conclusions formulated in the (OECD, 2018[13]) report on the dynamic interplay between national IP regimes, the level of resources devoted to enforcement systems, and the deterrents to counterfeiting.

References

OCDE (2008), *The Economic Impact of Counterfeiting and Piracy*, Éditions OCDE, Paris, https://doi.org/10.1787/9789264045521-en. [9]

OCDE/EUIPO (2021), *Misuse of Containerized Maritime Shipping in the Global Trade of Counterfeits*, Éditions OCDE, Paris,, https://doi.org/10.1787/e39d8939-en. [8]

OECD (2021), *COVID-19 vaccine and the Threat of Illicit Trade, Chair's Summary Note*, https://www.oecd.org/gov/illicit-trade/summary-note-covid-19-vaccine-and-the-threat-of-illicit-trade.pdf. [12]

OECD (2020), *Illicit Trade in a Time of Crisis. Chair's Summary Note*, https://www.oecd.org/gov/illicit-trade/oecd-webinar-illicit-trade-time-crisis-23-april.pdf. [10]

OECD (2020), *Trade in Fake Medicines at the Time of the Covid-19 Pandemics. Chair's Summary Note*, https://www.oecd.org/gov/illicit-trade/oecd-fake-medicines-webinar-june-10-summary-note.pdf. [14]

OECD (2018), *Governance Frameworks to Counter Illicit Trade*, OECD Publishing, Paris,, https://doi.org/10.1787/9789264291652-en. [13]

OECD/EUIPO (2020), *Trade in Counterfeit Pharmaceutical Products*, Illicit Trade, OECD Publishing, Paris, https://dx.doi.org/10.1787/a7c7e054-en. [7]

OECD/EUIPO (2019), *Trends in Trade in Counterfeit and Pirated Goods*, OECD Publishing, Paris,, https://doi.org/10.1787/g2g9f533-en. [3]

OECD/EUIPO (2018), *Misuse of Small Parcels for Trade in Counterfeit Goods: Facts and Trends*, OECD Publishing, Paris, https://doi.org/10.1787/9789264307858-en. [6]

OECD/EUIPO (2018), *Trade in Counterfeit Goods and Free Trade Zones: Evidence from Recent Trends*, OECD Publishing, Paris/EUIPO, Alicante, https://doi.org/10.1787/9789264289550-en. [4]

OECD/EUIPO (2018), *Why Do Countries Export Fakes?: The Role of Governance Frameworks, Enforcement and Socio-economic Factors*, OECD Publishing, Paris/EUIPO, Alicante, https://doi.org/10.1787/9789264302464-en. [5]

OECD/EUIPO (2017), *Mapping the Real Routes of Trade in Fake Goods, Illicit Trade*, OECD Publishing, Paris, https://doi.org/10.1787/9789264278349-en. [2]

OECD/EUIPO (2016), *Trade in Counterfeit and Pirated Goods: Mapping the Economic Impact, Illicit Trade*, OECD Publishing, Paris, https://doi.org/10.1787/9789264252653-en. [1]

UNICRI (2020), *"Cyber-crime during the COVID-19 Pandemic"*, http://www.unicri.it/news/cyber-crime-during-covid-19-pandemic. [11]

Annex A. Methodological notes

A.1. Constructing the General Trade-Related Index of Counterfeiting for products (GTRIC-p)

GTRIC-p is constructed through four steps:

1. For each reporting economy, the seizure percentages for sensitive goods are calculated.

2. For each product category, aggregate seizure percentages are calculated, taking the reporting economies' share of total sensitive imports as weights.

3. From these, a counterfeit source factor is established for each industry, based on the industries' weight in terms of total trade.

4. Based on these factors, the GTRIC-p is calculated.

Step 1: Measuring reporter-specific product seizure intensities

$\tilde{v}_i^k$ and $\tilde{m}_i^k$ are, respectively, the seizure and import values of product type k (as registered according to the HS on the two-digit level) in economy i from *any* provenance economy in a given year. Economy i's relative seizure intensity (seizure percentages) of good k, denoted below as γ_i^k is then defined as:

$$\gamma_i^k = \frac{\tilde{v}_i^k}{\sum_{k=1}^{\bar{K}} \tilde{v}_i^k}, \text{ such that } \sum_{k=1}^{\bar{K}} \gamma_i^k = 1 \ \forall \ i \ \in \{1, \dots, \bar{N}\}$$

$k = \{1, \dots, \bar{K}\}$ is the range of sensitive goods (the total number of goods is given by K) and $i = \{1, \dots, \bar{N}\}$ is the range of reporting economies (the total number of economies is given by N).

Step 2: Measuring general product seizure intensities

The general seizure intensity for product k, denoted Γ^k, is then determined by averaging seizure intensities, γ_i^k, weighted by the reporting economies' share of total sensitive imports in a given product category, k. Hence:

$$\Gamma^k = \sum_{i=1}^{\bar{N}} \omega_i \gamma_i^k \ , \ \forall \ k \ \in \{1, \dots, \bar{K}\}$$

The weight of reporting economy i is given by:

$$\omega_i = \frac{\widetilde{m}_i^k}{\sum_{i=1}^{\bar{N}} \widetilde{m}_i^k}$$

where $\widetilde{m}_i$ is i's total registered import value of sensitive goods ($\sum_{i=1}^{\bar{n}} \omega_i = 1$)

Step 3: Measuring product-specific counterfeiting factors

$\widetilde{M}_i^k = \sum_{i=1}^{N} \widetilde{m}_i^k$ is defined as the total registered imports of sensitive good k for *all* economies and $\widetilde{M} = \sum_{k=1}^{\bar{K}} M^k$ is defined as the total registered world imports of *all* sensitive goods.

The world import share of good k, denoted s^k, is therefore given by:

$$s^k = \frac{\widetilde{M}^k}{\widetilde{M}}, \text{ such that } \sum_{k=1}^{\bar{K}} s^k = 1$$

The general counterfeiting factor of product category k, denoted CP^k, is then determined as the following:

$$CP^k = \frac{\Gamma^k}{s^k}$$

The counterfeiting factor reflects the sensitivity of product infringements occurring in a particular product category, relative to its share in international trade. These are based on the seizure percentages calculated for each reporting economy and constitute the foundation of the formation of GTRIC-p.

Step 4: Establishing GTRIC-p

GTRIC-p is constructed from a transformation of the general counterfeiting factor and measures the relative likelihood that different product categories will be subject to counterfeiting and piracy in international trade. The transformation of the counterfeiting factor is based on two main assumptions:

- Assumption (A1): The counterfeiting factor of a particular product category is positively correlated with the actual intensity of international trade in counterfeit and pirated goods covered by that chapter. The counterfeiting factors must thus reflect the real intensity of actual counterfeit trade in the given product categories.
- Assumption (A2): This acknowledges that the assumption A1 may not be entirely correct. For instance, the fact that infringing goods are detected more frequently in certain categories could imply that differences in counterfeiting factors across products merely reflect that some goods are easier to detect than others or that some goods, for one reason or another, have been specially targeted for inspection. The counterfeiting factors of product categories with lower counterfeiting factors could, therefore, underestimate actual counterfeiting and piracy intensities in these cases.

In accordance with assumption A1 (positive correlation between counterfeiting factors and actual infringement activities) and assumption A2 (lower counterfeiting factors may underestimate actual activities), GTRIC-p is established by applying a positive monotonic transformation of the counterfeiting factor index using natural logarithms. This standard technique of linearisation of a non-linear relationship (in the case of this study between counterfeiting factors and actual infringement activities) allows the index to be flattened and gives a higher relative weight to lower counterfeiting factors (Verbeek, 2000[14]).

In order to address the possibility of outliers at both ends of the counterfeiting factor index (i.e. some categories may be measured as particularly susceptible to infringement even though they are not, whereas others may be measured as insusceptible although they are), it is assumed that GTRIC-p follows a left-truncated normal distribution, with GTRIC-p only taking values of zero or above.

The transformed counterfeiting factor is defined as:

$$cp^k = \ln(CP^k + 1)$$

Assuming that the transformed counterfeiting factor can be described by a left-truncated normal distribution with $cp^k \geq 0$, then, following Hald (Hald, 1952[15]), the density function of GTRIC-p is given by:

$$f_{LTN}(cp^k) = \begin{cases} 0 & if\ cp^k \leq 0 \\ \dfrac{f(cp^k)}{\int_0^\infty f(cp^k)dcp^k} & if\ cp^k \geq 0 \end{cases}$$

where $f(cp^k)$ is the non-truncated normal distribution for cp^k specified as:

$$f(cp^k) = \frac{1}{\sqrt{2\pi\sigma_{cp}^2}}\ exp\left(-\frac{1}{2}\left(\frac{(cp^k) - \mu_{cp}}{\sigma_{cp}}\right)^2\right)$$

The mean and variance of the normal distribution, here denoted μ_{cp} and σ_{cp}^2, are estimated over the transformed counterfeiting factor index, cp^k, and given by $\hat{\mu}_{cp}^2$ and σ_{cp}^2. This enables the calculation of the counterfeit import propensity index (GTRIC-p) across HS codes, corresponding to the cumulative distribution function of cp^k.

A.2. Constructing the general trade-related index of counterfeiting economies (GTRIC-e)

GTRIC-e is also constructed through four steps:

1. For each reporting economy, the seizure percentages for provenance economies are calculated.
2. For each provenance economy, aggregate seizure percentages are calculated, taking the reporting economies' share of total sensitive imports as weights.
3. From these, each economy's counterfeit source factor is established, based on the provenance economies' weight in terms of total trade.
4. Based on these factors, the GTRIC-e is calculated.

Step 1: Measuring reporter-specific seizure intensities from each provenance economy

$\tilde{v}_i^j$ is economy i's registered seizures of all types of infringing goods (i.e. all k) originating from economy j in a given year in terms of their value. γ_i^j is economy i's relative seizure intensity (seizure percentage) of all infringing items that originate from economy j, in a given year:

$$\gamma_i^j = \frac{\tilde{v}_i^j}{\sum_{j=1}^{\bar{J}}\tilde{v}_i^j} \text{ such that } \sum_{j=1}^{\bar{J}}\gamma_i^j = 1\ \forall\ i\ \in \{1,...,\bar{N}\}$$

Where $j = \{1, ..., \bar{J}\}$ is the range of identified provenance economies (the total number of exporters is given by J) and $i = \{1, ..., \bar{N}\}$ is the range of reporting economies (the total number of economies is given by N).

Step 2: Measuring general seizure intensities of each provenance economy

The general seizure intensity for economy j, denoted Γ^j, is then determined by averaging seizure intensities, γ_i^j, weighted by the reporting economy's share of total imports from known counterfeit and pirate origins.[1] Hence:

$$\Gamma^j = \sum_{i=1}^{\bar{N}} \omega_i \gamma_i^j , \ \forall \ J \in \{1, ..., \bar{J}\}$$

The weight of reporting economy i is given by:

$$\omega_i = \frac{\tilde{m}_i^j}{\sum_{i=1}^{\bar{N}} \tilde{m}_i^j}, \text{ such that } \sum_{i=1}^{\bar{N}} \omega_i = 1$$

Step 3: Measuring partner-specific counterfeiting factors

$\bar{M}_i^j = \sum_{i=1}^{N} \bar{m}_i^j$ is defined as the total registered world imports of all sensitive products from j,[2] and $\bar{M} = \sum_{j=1}^{J} \bar{M}^j$ is the total world import of sensitive goods from all provenance economies.

The share of imports from provenance economy j in total world imports of sensitive goods, denoted s^j, is then given by:

$$s^j = \frac{\bar{M}^j}{\bar{M}}, \text{ such that } \sum_{j=1}^{\bar{J}} s^j = 1$$

From this, the economy-specific counterfeiting factor is established by dividing the general seizure intensity for economy j by the share of total imports of sensitive goods from j.

$$CE^j = \frac{\Gamma^j}{s^j}$$

Step 4: Establishing GTRIC-e

Gauging the magnitude of counterfeiting and piracy from a provenance economy perspective can be done in a similar fashion as for sensitive goods. Hence, a General Trade-Related Index of Counterfeiting for economies (GTRIC-e) is established along similar lines and assumptions:

- Assumption (A3): The intensity by which any counterfeit or pirated article from a particular economy is detected and seized by customs is positively correlated with the actual amount of counterfeit and pirate articles imported from that location.
- Assumption (A4): This acknowledges that assumption A3 may not be entirely correct. For instance, a high seizure intensity of counterfeit or pirated articles from a particular provenance economy could be an indication that the provenance economy is part of a customs profiling scheme or that it is specially targeted for investigation by customs. The importance that provenance economies with low seizure intensities play regarding actual counterfeiting and piracy activity could, therefore, be under-represented by the index and lead to an underestimation of the scale of counterfeiting and piracy.

As with the product-specific index, GTRIC-e is established by applying a positive monotonic transformation of the counterfeiting factor index for provenance economies using natural logarithms. This follows from assumption A3 (positive correlation between seizure intensities and actual infringement activities) and assumption A4 (lower intensities tend to underestimate actual activities). Considering the possibilities of outliers at both ends of the GTRIC e-distribution (i.e. some economies may be wrongly measured as being particularly susceptible sources of counterfeit and pirated imports, and vice versa), GTRIC-e is approximated by a left-truncated normal distribution as it does not take values below zero.

The transformed general counterfeiting factor across provenance economies on which GTRIC-e is based is therefore given by applying logarithms onto economy-specific general counterfeit factors (see, for example, Verbeek (Verbeek, 2000[14])):

$$ce^j = ln(CE^j + 1)$$

In addition, following GTRIC-p, it is assumed that GTRIC-e follows a truncated normal distribution with $ce^j \geq 0$ for all j. Following Hald (Hald, 1952[15]), the density function of the left-truncated normal distribution for ce^j is given by:

$$g_{LTN}(ce^j) = \begin{cases} 0 & if\ ce^j \leq 0 \\ \dfrac{g(ce^j)}{\int_0^\infty g(ce^j)dce} & if\ ce^j \geq 0 \end{cases}$$

where $g(ce^j)$ is the non-truncated normal distribution for ce^j specified as:

$$g(ce^j) = \frac{1}{\sqrt{2\pi\sigma_{ce}^2}} exp\left(-\frac{1}{2}\left(\frac{ce^j - \mu_{ce}}{\sigma_{ce}}\right)^2\right)$$

The mean and variance of the normal distribution, here denoted μ_{ce} and σ_{ce}^2, are estimated over the transformed counterfeiting factor index, ce^j, and given by $\hat{\mu}_{ce}$ and $\hat{\sigma}_{ce}^2$. This enables the calculation of the counterfeit import propensity index (GTRIC-e) across provenance economies, corresponding to the cumulative distribution function of ce^j.

A.3. Constructing the General Trade-Related Index of Counterfeiting (GTRIC)

In the (OECD/EUIPO, 2016[1]) and (OECD/EUIPO, 2019[3]) studies, propensities to import infringing goods from different trading partners were developed using seizure data as a basis. The use of data is maximised by applying a generalised approach in which the propensities for products to be counterfeit and for economies to be sources of counterfeit goods were analysed separately. This increased the data coverage of both products and provenance economies significantly, which increases the robustness of the overall estimation results. Unfortunately, it also reduced the detail of the analysis, meaning that counterfeit trade patterns specific to individual reporting economies, for both product types and trading partners, were not simultaneously accounted for; this introduced bias into the results. On balance, however, given the large scope of the analysis, the advantages of increasing data coverage can be viewed as outweighing the biases.

This approach combines the two indices: GTRIC-p and GTRIC-e. In this regard, it is important to emphasise that the index resulting from this combination does not account for differences in infringement intensities across different types of goods that may exist between economies. For instance, imports of certain counterfeit and pirated goods could be particularly large from some trading partners and small from others. An index taking such "infringement specialisation", or concentration, into account is desirable and possible to construct; but it would require detailed seizure data. The combined index, denoted GTRIC, is, therefore, a generalised index that approximates the relative likelihoods that particular product types, imported from specific trading partners, are counterfeit and/or pirated.

Establishing likelihoods for product and provenance economy

In this step, for each trade flow from a given provenance economy and for a given product category the likelihoods of containing counterfeit and pirated products will be established.

The general propensity for an economy to export infringed items of HS category k is denoted P^k, and given by GTRIC-p, so that:

$$P^k = F_{LTN}(cp^k)$$

where $F_{LTN}(cp^k)$ is the cumulative probability function of $f_{LTN}(cp^k)$.

Furthermore, the general likelihood of importing any type of infringing goods from economy j is denoted as P^j , and given by GTRIC-e, so that:

$$P^j = G_{LTN}(ce^j)$$

where $G_{LTN}(ce^j)$ is the cumulative probability function of $f_{LTN}(ce^j)$.

The general probability of importing counterfeit or pirated items of type k originating from economy j is then denoted P^{jk} and approximated by:

$$P^{jk} = P^k P^j$$

Therefore, $P^{jk} \in [\varepsilon_p \varepsilon_e; 1)$, $\forall j, k$, with $\varepsilon_p \varepsilon_e$ denoting the minimum average counterfeit export rate for each sensitive product category and each provenance economy,[3] it is assumed that $\varepsilon_p = \varepsilon_e = 0.05$.

A.4. Calculating the absolute value

α is the fixed point, i.e. the maximum average counterfeit import rate of a given type of infringing good, k, originating from a given trading partner, j.

α can be applied to propensities for importing infringing goods of type j from trading partner k (αP^{jk}). As a result, a matrix of counterfeit import propensities **C** is obtained.

$$C = \begin{pmatrix} \alpha P^{11} & \alpha P^{21} & & \alpha P^{1K} \\ \alpha P^{12} & \ddots & & \\ \vdots & & \alpha P^{jk} & \vdots \\ & & & \ddots \\ \alpha P^{J1} & & & \alpha P^{JK} \end{pmatrix} \text{ with dimension } J \times K$$

The matrix of world imports is denoted by **M**. Applying **C** on **M** yields the absolute volume of trade in counterfeit and pirated goods.

In particular, the import matrix **M** is given by:

$$M = \begin{pmatrix} M_1 \\ \vdots \\ M_i \\ \vdots \\ M_n \end{pmatrix} \text{ with dimension } n \times J \times K$$

Each element is defined by economy i's unique import matrix of good k from trading partner j.

$$M_i = \begin{pmatrix} m_{i1}^1 & m_{i1}^2 & & m_{i1}^K \\ m_{i2}^1 & \ddots & & \\ \vdots & & m_{ij}^k & \vdots \\ & & & \ddots & \\ m_{ij}^1 & & & m^{JK} \end{pmatrix} \quad \text{with dimension } J \times K$$

Hence, the element m_{ij}^k denotes i's imports of product category k from trading partner j, where $i = \{1,\dots,n\}$, $j = \{1,\dots,J\}$, and $k = \{1,\dots,K\}$.

Denoted by Ψ, the product-by-economy percentage of counterfeit and pirated imports can be determined as the following:

$$\Psi = C'M \div M$$

Total trade in counterfeit and pirated goods, denoted by the scalar **TC**, is then given by:

$$TC = i_1' \Psi i_2$$

where i_1 is a vector of one with dimension $nJ \times 1$, and i_2 is a vector of one with dimension $K \times 1$. Then, by denoting total world trade by the scalar $TM = i_1' M i_2$, the value of counterfeiting and piracy in world trade, s_{TC}, is determined by:

$$s_{TC} = \frac{TC}{TM}$$

A.5. Construction of RCAP-e and RCAT-e

Relative comparative advantage for production of a given good (RCAP-e)

The first statistical filter that can be used to tell producers from transit points looks at the production capacities of a given economy in a given sector. The rationale behind this test is simple: production activity often relies on certain skills, or resources. It also exhibits certain returns to scale properties that results in specialisation of this particular economy in the production of that good. Hence, production of counterfeits in a sector is more likely to occur in a known provenance economy that specialises in the legitimate production of a given good, than in a country without production capacity in a given sector.

This specialisation of a given trading economy in production of a given good is captured by an indicator of the relative comparative advantage for production (RCAP-e). The indicator looks at the share of industrial activity in a given sector with the total industrial activity in a given economy.

Construction of this indicator is based on industry statistics. Importantly, these statistics are based on a different taxonomy than the trade statistics, hence a matching exercise was performed (see Box B.1). A detailed description of the methodology used to calculate the RCAP-e is provided below.

Box A.1. Product classification methods

Although the datasets on trade and industrial activity in principle classify the same goods, they differ in the taxonomies used. Industry data (output) are extracted from the industrial statistics database of the United Nations Industrial Development Organization (UNIDO). These data are classified according to the categories of industrial activity (ISIC-Rev3) at a two-digit level. Trade data and seizure data are classified using the Harmonized Tariff Schedule (HTS) classification scheme. These differences are due to the fact that although they cover the same issues, they were created and are run independently.

In order to create the RCAP-e indicator, the HS code that refers to the GTRIC-p tables and to categories of international trade are matched with the relevant categories of industrial activity (ISIC). This is done following the concordance tables proposed by the United Nations Statistics Division (available at: http://unstats.un.org/unsd/cr/registry/regot.asp?Lg=1).

More formally, the revealed comparative advantage in production for an economy e in a given product category p (RCAP-e) measures whether this economy produces more of this given type of product as a share of its total production than the "average" country:

$$RCAP_{ep} = \frac{y_{ep} / \sum_p y_{ep}}{\sum_e y_{ep} / \sum_e \sum_p y_{ep}}$$

where y_{ep} is the output of product p by economy e in a given year.

Relative comparative advantage for being a transit point (RCAT-e).

The relative comparative advantage for being a transit point in global trade (RCAT-e) is the second filter used to determine the actual role of a provenance economy. This indicator represents the degree to which a given economy specialises in re-exporting a given product, e.g. through development of advanced logistical infrastructure, or by its convenient geographical location. Consequently, it is assumed that such factors that facilitate transiting of genuine products will also facilitate transit of fake products in the same product categories.

The RCAT-e indicator is calculated by comparing relative volumes of re-export of a given good to the shares calculated for other exporting economies. This is done based on re-export data that come from the UN Comtrade database. A detailed description of the methodology used to calculate the RCAT-e is provided in Annex B.

Formally, the revealed comparative advantage in transit for an economy e within a given product category p (RCAP-e) measures whether this economy re-exports more goods of this given type of product as a share of its total re-exports than the "average" country:

$$RCAT_{ep} = \frac{x_{ep} / \sum_p x_{ep}}{\sum_e x_{ep} / \sum_e \sum_p x_{ep}}$$

where x_{ep} is re-exports of product p by economy e in a given year.

Application of both filters

Once the statistical filters (RCAP-e and RCAT-e indicators) are constructed, they are applied to distinguish the producing economies from the key potential transit points. Both filters are applied for every economy on the top provenance list for counterfeit goods, i.e. economies with a high GTRIC-e score. The selection of top economies is done arbitrarily, depending on the distribution of the GTRIC within a given product category.

The rationale for using the filters is as follows: if an economy is not a significant producer of a fake good (i.e. its RCAP-e for this good is low) and/or is a large re-exporter of this good in legitimate trade (i.e its RCAT-e for this good is high), then it is likely to be a transit point.

On the other hand, if this top listed provenance economy of counterfeit goods within the product category is a significant producer (i.e. has a high RCAP-e score) or is a small re-exporter (i.e. has a low RCAT-e score), it is likely to be a producer of the fake goods.

This exercise results in a list of producers and a list of transit points. Together with the information on the place of seizure, this will allow the development of maps of trade in fake goods in given product categories, showing key producers, main transit point and main destination points.

References

Hald, A. (1952), *Statistical Theory with Engineering Applications, John Wiley and Sons, New York.*. [15]

OCDE (2008), *The Economic Impact of Counterfeiting and Piracy*, Éditions OCDE, Paris, https://doi.org/10.1787/9789264045521-en. [9]

OCDE/EUIPO (2021), *Misuse of Containerized Maritime Shipping in the Global Trade of Counterfeits*, Éditions OCDE, Paris,, https://doi.org/10.1787/e39d8939-en. [8]

OECD (2021), *COVID-19 vaccine and the Threat of Illicit Trade, Chair's Summary Note*, https://www.oecd.org/gov/illicit-trade/summary-note-covid-19-vaccine-and-the-threat-of-illicit-trade.pdf. [12]

OECD (2020), *Illicit Trade in a Time of Crisis. Chair's Summary Note*, https://www.oecd.org/gov/illicit-trade/oecd-webinar-illicit-trade-time-crisis-23-april.pdf. [10]

OECD (2020), *Trade in Fake Medicines at the Time of the Covid-19 Pandemics. Chair's Summary Note*, https://www.oecd.org/gov/illicit-trade/oecd-fake-medicines-webinar-june-10-summary-note.pdf. [16]

OECD (2018), *Governance Frameworks to Counter Illicit Trade*, OECD Publishing, Paris,, https://doi.org/10.1787/9789264291652-en. [13]

OECD/EUIPO (2020), *Trade in Counterfeit Pharmaceutical Products*, Illicit Trade, OECD Publishing, Paris, https://dx.doi.org/10.1787/a7c7e054-en. [7]

OECD/EUIPO (2019), *Trends in Trade in Counterfeit and Pirated Goods*, OECD Publishing, Paris,, https://doi.org/10.1787/g2g9f533-en. [3]

OECD/EUIPO (2018), *Misuse of Small Parcels for Trade in Counterfeit Goods: Facts and Trends*, OECD Publishing, Paris, https://doi.org/10.1787/9789264307858-en. [6]

OECD/EUIPO (2018), *Trade in Counterfeit Goods and Free Trade Zones: Evidence from Recent Trends*, OECD Publishing, Paris/EUIPO, Alicante, https://doi.org/10.1787/9789264289550-en. [4]

OECD/EUIPO (2018), *Why Do Countries Export Fakes?: The Role of Governance Frameworks, Enforcement and Socio-economic Factors*, OECD Publishing, Paris/EUIPO, Alicante, https://doi.org/10.1787/9789264302464-en. [5]

OECD/EUIPO (2017), *Mapping the Real Routes of Trade in Fake Goods, Illicit Trade*, OECD Publishing, Paris, https://doi.org/10.1787/9789264278349-en. [2]

OECD/EUIPO (2016), *Trade in Counterfeit and Pirated Goods: Mapping the Economic Impact, Illicit Trade*, OECD Publishing, Paris, https://doi.org/10.1787/9789264252653-en. [1]

UNICRI (2020), *"Cyber-crime during the COVID-19 Pandemic"*, http://www.unicri.it/news/cyber-crime-during-covid-19-pandemic. [11]

Verbeek, M. (2000), *A Guide to Modern Econometrics, Wiley.*. [14]

Notes

[1] This is different to the economy's share of total imports of sensitive goods used to calculate GTRIC-p.

[2] This is different to the total imports of sensitive goods as used in calculation of GTRIC-p.

[3] In the OECD methodology, these factors were applied to all provenance economies and all HS modules in order to account for counterfeit and pirated exports of products and/or from provenance economies that were not identified. This assumption is relaxed in this study, given the overall good data quality.

Annex B. Additional tables

Table B.1. GTRIC-e, RCAP-e and RCAT-e for perfumery and cosmetics

Average 2017-2019

Provenance	GTRICe world	GTRIC-e EU	RCAPe	RCATe
Algeria	0.25	0.33		
Bahrain	0.38	0.33		0.26
Belarus	0.18	0.75	0.00	
Belgium	0.06		2.15	
Brazil	0.06		0.00	
Brunei Darussalam	0.13	0.33		0.03
Bulgaria	0.34	0.63	2.73	
Cambodia	0.33			
Cameroon	0.08	0.33		
Canada	0.17	0.05	1.31	1.54
China (People's Republic of)	1.00	1.00		
Colombia	0.12		9.03	
Czech Republic	0.11			
Denmark	0.06		1.14	
Dominican Republic	0.11			
Ecuador	0.06	0.05	4.23	
Egypt	0.13	0.24		
Ethiopia	0.33	0.33		0.04
North Macedonia	0.32	0.33		
France	0.11		5.59	
Georgia	0.08			1.70
Germany	0.17		1.45	
Greece	0.06	0.07	2.35	
Hong Kong (China)	1.00	1.00		
Hungary	0.11	0.05	0.85	
India	1.00	0.15	2.28	
Indonesia	0.13		0.00	
Iran	0.12	0.16		
Israel	0.17	0.15	0.00	
Italy	0.17		1.83	0.52
Jordan	0.50			1.12
Korea	0.05	0.05		
Kuwait	0.97	0.63		1.36
Lao People's Democratic Republic	0.08	0.33		0.30
Lebanon	0.70	0.27		
Malaysia	0.18	0.80	0.00	
Mali	0.33	0.33		
Malta	0.06	0.05	0.00	
Montenegro	0.33		0.00	
Morocco	0.05	0.05		

Provenance	GTRIC-e world	GTRIC-e EU	RCAP-e	RCAT-e
Netherlands	0.17	0.10	0.67	
Nicaragua	0.33	0.33		
Nigeria	0.48			
Pakistan	0.10			0.02
Panama	0.62		2.09	
Peru	0.33		4.21	
Philippines	0.13	0.07	4.36	
Poland	0.14	0.05	2.21	
Romania	0.05		0.70	
Russia	0.18	0.51		
Saudi Arabia	0.16	0.67	2.64	0.88
Serbia	0.12	0.28	0.00	
Singapore	0.18	0.87	2.52	
Solomon Islands	0.33	0.33		
South Africa	0.16			0.25
Spain	0.11		2.87	0.00
Swaziland	0.05	0.05		
Sweden	0.05	0.04	0.61	
Switzerland	0.17	0.15	0.00	
Syrian Arab Republic	0.07	0.11		
Thailand	0.17	0.18		3.03
Tonga	0.33	0.33		
Turkey	0.94	1.00	1.69	
Ukraine	0.20	0.63	1.11	
United Arab Emirates	0.96	1.00	0.00	2.03
United Kingdom	0.17	0.10	1.74	0.25
United States	0.17	0.15		0.58
Venezuela	0.50	1.00		
Viet Nam	0.18	0.26		

Table B.2. GTRIC-e, RCAP-e and RCAT-e for leather articles and handbags

Average 2017-2019

Povenance	GTRIC-e world	GTRIC-e EU	RCAP-e	RCAT-e
Afghanistan	1.00	0.67	0.60	0.19
Albania	0.45	0.78	0.00	
Algeria	0.33	0.33		
Argentina	0.23	0.09		
Armenia	0.41	0.64	0.49	1.03
Australia	0.13	0.15	0.00	
Austria	0.13	0.06	0.40	
Azerbaijan	0.66	0.67	0.06	
Bahrain	1.00	1.00		2.61
Bangladesh	0.06			
Belarus	0.19	0.66	0.00	
Bolivia	0.08			0.45
Bosnia and Herzegovina	0.21	0.20	1.65	
Brazil	0.21	0.25	0.50	
British Virgin Islands	0.67			
Bulgaria	0.52	0.62	1.80	
Cambodia	0.21	0.19		
Cameroon	1.00	0.67		
Canada	0.36	0.23	0.04	1.91
Chile	0.14			
China (People's Republic of)	0.74	0.82	1.91	
Colombia	0.70	0.85	2.11	
Costa Rica	0.08	0.33		
Croatia	0.07		2.56	
Democratic Republic of the Congo	0.67	0.33		0.00
Denmark	0.15		0.25	
Dominican Republic	0.93	0.60		
Ecuador	0.84	0.33	0.00	
Egypt	1.00	1.00		
El Salvador	0.07			
Estonia	0.13	0.12	0.74	0.43
Ethiopia	0.08	0.24		5.70
North Macedonia	0.28	0.48		
France	0.20	0.12	10.87	
Georgia	0.16	0.33	0.10	0.18
Germany	0.20	0.12	0.42	
Ghana	0.58	0.67		
Gibraltar	0.33			
Greece	0.40	0.26	0.71	
Guatemala	0.07			
Guinea	0.33			
Honduras	0.38			
Hong Kong (China)	1.00	1.00		
India	0.20	0.18		
Indonesia	0.20	0.20		
Iran	0.98	1.00		
Iraq	1.00	0.33	0.07	
Israel	0.14	0.12	0.26	
Italy	0.20	0.06	17.44	0.17

Provenance	GTRIC-e world	GTRIC-e EU	RCAP-e	RCAT-e
Japan	0.27	0.45		
Jordan	1.00	0.33		0.41
Kazakhstan	0.60	0.67	0.03	
Kenya	0.94	0.67	0.00	0.06
Korea	0.44	0.46		
Kuwait	0.59	0.87		0.81
Lao People's Democratic Republic	1.00			0.16
Latvia	0.08		0.00	
Lebanon	0.69	0.84		
Lithuania	0.51		0.57	
Macau (China)	0.06			17.25
Madagascar	0.17	0.25		0.05
Malaysia	0.36	0.92		
Mauritania	0.25	0.33		
Mexico	0.29	0.06	0.40	
Moldova	0.08	0.11	5.81	6.50
Mongolia	0.33		0.00	
Morocco	0.62	0.94		
Myanmar	0.13	0.06	0.00	0.00
Netherlands	0.20	0.18	0.00	
New Zealand	0.13	0.33	0.00	4.42
Nicaragua	0.14	0.38		
Nigeria	1.00	1.00		
Oman	0.21		0.00	0.43
Pakistan	0.27	0.19		0.21
Peru	0.15	0.26	0.37	
Philippines	0.28	0.54		
Poland	0.20		2.43	
Portugal	0.06	0.06	1.69	
Qatar	0.47	0.81	0.00	0.59
Romania	0.06		3.74	
Russia	0.91	1.00	0.00	
San Marino	0.33	0.33		
Saudi Arabia	0.73	0.58	0.05	0.32
Senegal	1.00	1.00		
Serbia	0.26	0.37	0.00	
Singapore	0.63	1.00	0.00	
Sint Maarten	0.33			
Spain	0.20	0.18	2.73	0.01
Sri Lanka	0.15	0.06		0.00
Suriname	0.24	0.33		0.13
Sweden	0.14	0.07	0.50	
Switzerland	0.20	0.19	0.00	
Syrian Arab Republic	0.64	0.67		
Thailand	0.42	0.72		0.60
Togo	0.33			
Tokelau	0.33			
Tunisia	0.20	0.19		
Turkey	1.00	1.00	1.97	
Uganda	0.63	0.33		0.09
Ukraine	0.38	0.65	0.19	
United Arab Emirates	0.92	1.00	0.00	1.07

Provenance	GTRIC-e world	GTRIC-e EU	RCAP-e	RCAT-e
United Kingdom	0.22	0.06	1.38	0.48
United States	0.20	0.27	0.53	0.98
Venezuela	1.00	0.33		
Viet Nam	0.22	0.20		

Table B.3. GTRIC-e, RCAP-e and RCAT-e for footwear

Average 2017-2019

Provenance	GTRIC-e world	GTRIC-e EU	RCAP-e	RCAT-e
Afghanistan	1.00	0.67		2.80
Albania	0.23	0.24		
Algeria	0.67	0.67		
Argentina	0.15			
Armenia	0.55	1.00	0.38	
Australia	0.21	0.29	0.59	
Austria	0.13	0.13	0.80	
Azerbaijan	0.15	0.33	0.29	
Bahamas	0.33			
Bahrain	0.98	0.67		3.10
Bangladesh	0.21	0.08	6.34	
Belarus	0.13	0.23		
Belgium	0.14	0.13	0.05	
Benin	0.17	0.33		0.01
Bhutan	0.33			
Bosnia and Herzegovina	0.14	0.13		
Brazil	0.15	0.20	3.62	
British Virgin Islands	0.33			
Bulgaria	0.17	0.16	1.32	
Burundi	0.33	0.33		0.04
Cambodia	0.14	0.06		
Cameroon	0.90	0.67		
Canada	0.36	0.20	0.09	2.09
Chile	0.20	0.33		
China (People's Republic of)	0.87	0.97		
Colombia	0.81	0.98	1.77	
Congo	0.33			
Croatia	0.13	0.13		
Denmark	0.15		0.05	
Dominica	0.15	0.33		
Dominican Republic	0.31	0.16		
Ecuador	0.24	1.00	1.44	
Egypt	0.75	0.72		
Estonia	0.14	0.14	0.74	0.90
Ethiopia	0.07	0.24		25.90
North Macedonia	0.14			
France	0.14		0.21	
Georgia	0.58	0.67	0.26	0.30
Germany	0.20	0.13	0.34	
Ghana	0.96	1.00		
Gibraltar	0.33			

Greece	0.73	0.69	0.63	
Guatemala	0.15			
Guinea	1.00	1.00		
Hong Kong (China)	1.00	1.00		
India	0.21	0.20	1.77	
Indonesia	0.20	0.20		
Iran	0.90	1.00		
Iraq	0.67	0.67	0.21	
Israel	0.22	0.71		
Italy	0.20	0.13	5.17	0.09
Japan	0.24	0.22		
Jordan	0.67	0.33		0.72
Kazakhstan	0.41	0.98	0.22	
Kenya	0.25	0.33		0.19
Korea	0.59	0.30		
Kuwait	0.41	0.09		1.64
Kyrgyzstan	0.08	0.33	0.65	
Lao People's Democratic Republic	0.07			0.11
Latvia	0.28		0.14	
Lebanon	0.95	1.00		
Libya	0.33	0.33		
Lithuania	0.25		0.17	
Luxembourg	0.18	0.17		17.65
Macau (China)	0.07	0.07		10.72
Malaysia	0.34	0.78	0.61	
Mauritania	0.67	0.67		
Mexico	0.21	0.07	1.44	
Moldova	0.07	0.08		7.56
Morocco	0.56	0.32		
Myanmar	0.07	0.06		0.00
Namibia	0.22	0.33		0.10
Nepal	0.07	0.19		
Netherlands	0.21	0.22		
New Zealand	0.07	0.07	0.00	3.83
Nicaragua	0.20	0.67		
Nigeria	1.00	1.00		
Oman	0.09		0.15	1.34
Pakistan	0.28	0.13		0.00
Panama	0.47			
Peru	0.07	0.11		
Philippines	0.26	0.24	0.94	
Poland	0.20		0.84	
Qatar	0.18	0.19	0.05	0.57
Romania	0.20		4.08	
Russia	0.31	1.00		
Rwanda	0.32	0.33		2.72
Saudi Arabia	0.48	0.59	0.11	0.32
Senegal	0.96	1.00		
Serbia	0.21	0.21		
Singapore	1.00	1.00	0.00	
South Africa	0.07	0.33		2.24
Spain	0.20	0.13	2.26	0.01
Sri Lanka	0.07		1.40	0.01

Suriname	0.33	0.33		0.10
Sweden	0.18	0.19	0.05	
Switzerland	0.23	0.21	0.46	
Syrian Arab Republic	0.48	1.00		
Tanzania	0.23	0.33		
Thailand	0.25	0.31		0.54
Togo	0.47	1.00		
Tunisia	0.21	0.13		
Turkey	0.99	1.00	2.06	
Uganda	0.26			0.32
Ukraine	0.24	0.25	0.92	
United Arab Emirates	1.00	0.99		1.87
United Kingdom	0.21	0.20	0.27	1.32
United States	0.23	0.33		0.53
Venezuela	1.00	0.67		
Viet Nam	0.21	0.20		

Table B.4. GTRIC-e, RCAP-e and RCAT-e for toys and games

Average 2017-2019

Provenance	GTRIC-e world	GTRIC-e EU	RCAP-e	RCAT-e
Argentina	0.67			
Armenia	0.15	0.32	0.05	0.01
Australia	0.26	0.14	1.39	
Austria	0.08	0.04	7.25	
Azerbaijan	0.33	0.33	0.63	
Bangladesh	0.08	0.04	0.54	
Belarus	0.00	0.05	0.00	
Brazil	0.08	0.06	1.03	
Bulgaria	0.24	0.13	12.78	
Canada	0.33	0.10	2.01	2.37
Chile	0.67	0.07	0.00	
China (People's Republic of)	0.69	0.92		
Ecuador	0.67	0.67	0.08	
Estonia	0.39	0.10	1.39	0.93
France	0.26		1.58	
Georgia	0.53	0.54	0.00	0.04
Germany	0.17	0.04	2.30	
Hong Kong (China)	1.00	1.00		
India	0.35	0.05	0.43	
Indonesia	0.29	0.17	0.00	
Iran	0.95	0.98		
Iraq	0.29	0.33	0.00	
Israel	0.15	0.10	2.16	
Japan	0.25	0.17		
Kazakhstan	0.09	0.14	0.11	
Korea	0.36	0.26		
Kuwait	0.33	0.33		0.34
Latvia	0.15	0.13	1.01	
Lebanon	0.10	0.19		
Luxembourg	0.08	0.05	0.24	0.93
Malaysia	0.25	0.18	0.75	
Malta	0.10		0.00	
Mexico	0.24	0.19	1.37	
Morocco	0.15	0.14		
Myanmar	0.08	0.05	0.00	0.00
Netherlands	0.24	0.15	0.00	
New Zealand	0.08	0.08	0.00	1.08
Norway	0.08	0.04	1.26	
Pakistan	0.28	0.15		0.03
Peru	0.33		0.00	
Philippines	0.16	0.11	1.71	
Russia	0.24	0.17		
Saudi Arabia	0.33	0.33	0.11	0.54
Singapore	0.87	1.00	0.00	
Spain	0.19	0.06	1.61	0.01
Suriname	0.33	0.33		0.07
Sweden	0.08	0.04	0.86	
Switzerland	0.25	0.16	0.38	
Syrian Arab Republic	0.33	0.33		

Provennace	GTRIC-e world	GTRIC-e EU	RCAP-e	RCAT-e
Thailand	0.31	0.48		0.36
Turkey	0.94	1.00	0.73	
Ukraine	0.24	0.15	0.83	
United Arab Emirates	0.98	0.37	0.00	0.58
United Kingdom	0.24		2.19	0.14
United States	0.26	0.14		1.26
Venezuela	0.10	0.33		
Viet Nam	0.16	0.10		

Table B.5. GTRIC-e, RCAP-e and RCAT-e for jewellery

Average 2017-2019

Provenance	GTRIC-e world	GTRIC-e EU	RCAP-e	RCAT-e
Afghanistan	0.03	0.16	0.00	
Albania	0.03	0.07	0.47	
Australia	0.03	0.07	0.21	
Azerbaijan	0.03		0.15	
Bahrain	0.34	0.30		0.27
Bangladesh	0.07	0.31	0.44	
Belarus	0.00	0.07	0.76	
Benin	0.08	0.67		0.74
Cambodia	0.07			
Cameroon	0.07	0.33		
Canada	0.09	0.15	0.22	0.17
Chile	0.11		0.10	
China (People's Republic of)	1.00	1.00		
Cocos (Keeling) Islands	0.00			
Colombia	0.24	0.06	0.10	
Costa Rica	0.33	0.33	0.00	
Democratic Republic of the Congo	0.03			0.00
Dominican Republic	0.06	0.07		
Ecuador	0.05	0.27	0.00	
Egypt	0.06	0.60	0.98	
Estonia	0.03	0.07	0.04	0.06
Ethiopia	0.08	0.33		0.00
Finland	0.03		0.10	
France	0.03		0.27	
Georgia	0.03	0.07	0.24	0.00
Germany	0.06	0.06	0.13	
Ghana	0.09	0.41		
Hong Kong (China)	1.00	1.00		
India	0.10	0.06	2.23	
Indonesia	0.06		0.91	
Iran	0.15	0.33		
Iraq	0.03	0.10	0.20	
Israel	0.06	0.14	0.52	
Italy	0.03		0.65	0.71
Japan	0.06	0.15	1.23	
Jordan	0.33	0.06	0.74	0.27
Korea	0.08			
Kuwait	0.10	0.58		0.28
Lao People's Democratic Republic	0.09			0.00
Latvia	0.07		0.01	
Lebanon	0.09	0.24		
Malaysia	0.17	0.92	0.34	
Mexico	0.19	0.06	0.04	
Morocco	0.08	0.28		
Myanmar	0.03	0.06	0.03	0.05
Netherlands	0.10	0.06	0.06	
Nigeria	0.07	0.22		
Oman	0.03	0.33	0.13	0.13
Pakistan	0.20			0.17

Provenance	GTRIC-e world	GTRIC-e EU	RCAP-e	RCAT-e
Panama	0.67	0.33	0.00	
Peru	0.03		5.08	
Philippines	0.16	0.30	0.05	
Qatar	0.10	0.61	0.02	0.67
Romania	0.04		0.12	
Russia	0.09	0.22		
Saudi Arabia	0.03		0.11	0.23
Senegal	0.12	0.33		
Singapore	0.36	0.39	0.30	
South Africa	0.03	0.06		0.74
Sri Lanka	0.06		0.27	0.01
Swaziland	0.03	0.24		
Switzerland	0.06	0.14	0.22	
Syrian Arab Republic	0.03	0.33		
Thailand	0.51	0.49	0.84	0.05
Turkey	0.49	0.99	0.68	
Tuvalu	0.33	0.33		
Uganda	0.03			0.04
Ukraine	0.14	0.42	0.04	
United Arab Emirates	0.09	0.29	0.65	1.87
United Kingdom	0.03	0.06	0.20	0.66
United States	0.09	0.22		0.84
Venezuela	0.03	0.07		
Viet Nam	0.53	0.48		

Table B.6. GTRIC-e, RCAP-e and RCAT-e for clothing

Average 2017-2019

Provenance	GTRIC-e world	GTRIC-e EU	RCAP-e	RCAT-e
Afghanistan	1.00	1.00	0.00	0.04
Albania	0.20	0.26	2.39	
Algeria	1.00	1.00		
Argentina	0.22	0.42		
Armenia	0.23	0.36	0.37	0.11
Australia	0.13	0.19	0.32	
Austria	0.00	0.08	0.74	
Azerbaijan	1.00	1.00	0.35	
Bahrain	0.19	0.59		0.14
Bangladesh	0.32	0.44	19.44	
Belarus	0.20	0.25	0.43	
Belgium	0.07	0.09	0.95	
Bhutan	0.19			
Bolivia	0.29	0.23		0.00
Bosnia and Herzegovina	0.19	0.16	19.99	
Brazil	0.34	0.49	0.42	
Bulgaria	0.36	0.34	2.86	
Burundi	0.26	0.33		0.02
Cambodia	0.13	0.16		
Cameroon	1.00	0.67		
Canada	0.22	0.25	0.26	1.78
Chile	0.28	0.81	0.12	
China (People's Republic of)	0.77	0.78		
Colombia	0.37	0.79	8.39	
Côte d'Ivoire	0.10	0.18		
Croatia	0.06	0.08	1.35	
Curaçao	0.67		0.00	
Cyprus	0.09	0.12	3.64	0.06
Czech Republic	0.07	0.09		
Democratic Republic of the Congo	0.33			0.00
Denmark	0.13		0.19	
Dominican Republic	0.34	0.09		
Ecuador	0.49	0.16	1.40	
Egypt	0.24	0.42	2.94	
El Salvador	0.13			
Estonia	0.19	0.24	0.56	1.16
Ethiopia	0.07	0.09		0.00
North Macedonia	0.25	0.26		
France	0.19	0.08	0.98	
Georgia	0.24	0.48	0.47	0.56
Germany	0.22	0.27	1.03	
Ghana	0.57	1.00		
Gibraltar	0.33			
Greece	0.36	0.25	2.57	
Guatemala	0.20			
Guinea	0.58	0.67		
Guyana	0.15	0.33		0.08
Haiti	0.07	0.09		
Honduras	0.20	0.17		

Provenance	GTRIC-e world	GTRIC-e EU	RCAP-e	RCAT-e
Hong Kong (China)	1.00	1.00		
Hungary	0.14	0.09	1.17	
Iceland	0.14	0.19	0.52	
India	0.36	0.30	3.03	
Indonesia	0.34	0.24	0.92	
Iran	1.00	1.00		
Iraq	1.00	1.00	0.99	
Israel	0.32	0.27	0.19	
Italy	0.21		2.92	0.32
Japan	0.20	0.25	0.00	
Jordan	0.20	0.31	2.38	18.04
Kazakhstan	0.23	0.63	1.15	
Kenya	0.40	0.99	0.65	0.07
Korea	0.31	0.29		
Kuwait	0.16	0.33		0.13
Kyrgyzstan	0.08	0.33	1.07	
Lao People's Democratic Republic	0.21	0.08		0.16
Latvia	0.08		3.61	
Lebanon	0.87	0.99		
Lesotho	0.06	0.10		
Liberia	0.32	0.33		
Libya	0.67	0.67		
Lithuania	0.16		5.74	
Luxembourg	0.13	0.17	0.35	0.27
Madagascar	0.46	0.59		51.28
Malaysia	0.22	0.31	0.16	
Mali	0.12	0.20		
Mauritius	0.06	0.08	5.99	
Mexico	0.25	0.18	0.31	
Moldova	0.21	0.28		31.90
Mongolia	0.08		2.06	
Montenegro	0.33	0.33	0.00	
Morocco	0.24	0.32		
Nepal	0.14	0.20	0.00	
Netherlands	0.19	0.24	11.50	
New Zealand	0.13	0.18	0.00	1.06
Nicaragua	0.13	0.22		
Nigeria	1.00	1.00		
Norway	0.16	0.25	0.14	
Pakistan	0.69	0.31		0.00
Panama	0.14	0.60	0.12	
Paraguay	0.14	0.65		
Peru	0.78	0.27	0.99	
Philippines	0.32	0.32	2.16	
Poland	0.13		0.46	
Portugal	0.28	0.38	9.73	
Qatar	0.39	0.64	0.47	0.02
Romania	0.13		4.48	
Russia	0.36	0.98		
Saudi Arabia	0.18	0.63	4.25	0.40
Senegal	1.00	1.00		
Serbia	0.13	0.17	0.67	

Provenance	GTRIC-e world	GTRIC-e EU	RCAP-e	RCAT-e
Singapore	0.87	1.00	0.12	
Slovenia	0.07		0.18	
Somalia	0.33			
South Africa	0.13	0.21		2.10
Spain	0.13	0.16	2.25	0.00
Sri Lanka	0.20	0.24	18.08	138.54
Sudan	0.30	0.33		
Suriname	0.32	0.33		0.01
Swaziland	0.06	0.32		
Sweden	0.13	0.16	1.08	
Switzerland	0.43	0.50	3.23	
Syrian Arab Republic	1.00	1.00		
Tanzania	0.20	0.50		
Thailand	0.42	0.62	2.81	0.38
Togo	0.23	0.67		
Tokelau	0.33	0.28		
Tunisia	0.20	0.26		
Turkey	0.94	0.96	15.94	
Uganda	0.99	0.29		0.00
Ukraine	0.31	0.43	0.26	
United Arab Emirates	0.86	0.96	0.44	1.24
United Kingdom	0.13	0.16	0.22	0.01
United States	0.26	0.75		0.72
Uruguay	0.07	0.16		
Uzbekistan	0.06	0.08	10.79	4.99
Venezuela	0.94	0.53		
Viet Nam	0.46	0.26